Plateau Indians

Plateau Indians

Craig A. Doherty
Katherine M. Doherty

CHELSEA HOUSE
PUBLISHERS
An imprint of Infobase Publishing

☖ ☖ ☖

Plateau Indians

Chelsea House
An imprint of Infobase Publishing
132 West 31st Street
New York NY 10001

Library of Congress Cataloging-in-Publication Data
Doherty, Craig A.
　Plateau Indians / Craig A. Doherty and Katherine M. Doherty.
　　p. cm. — (Native America)
　Includes bibliographical references and index.
　ISBN 978-0-8160-5971-3 (alk. paper)
　1. Indians of North America—West (U.S.)—History—Juvenile literature.
2. Indians of North America—West (U.S.)—Social life and customs—Juvenile literature. I. Doherty, Katherine M. II. Title. III. Series.
　E78.W5D65 2007
　978 .02—dc22　　　　　　　　　　　　2007013415

Chelsea House books are available at special discounts when purchased in bulk quantities for businesses, associations, institutions, or sales promotions. Please call our Special Sales Department in New York at (212) 967-8800 or (800) 322-8755.

You can find Chelsea House on the World Wide Web at
http://www.chelseahouse.com

Text design by Erika K. Arroyo
Cover design by Salvatore Luongo
Maps and graph by Sholto Ainslie

Printed in the United States of America

VB MSRF 10 9 8 7 6 5 4 3 2 1

This book is printed on acid-free paper.

Note on Photos

Many of the illustrations and photographs used in this book are old, historical images. The quality of the prints is not always up to modern standards, as in some cases the originals are damaged. The content of the illustrations, however, made their inclusion important despite problems in reproduction.

*This book is dedicated to the many students of all ages
we have worked with and taught over the years.*

❊ ❊ ❊

Craig and Katherine Doherty

❊ ❊ ❊

Contents

Introduction

Native American peoples live and have lived for millennia throughout the Americas. Many people think of Indians solely in the past tense, as part of history. While these groups have a long and interesting history, their contributions to American society have continued through the 20th century and into the 21st century. Native America today is an exciting place, with much waiting to be discovered. This series of books will introduce readers to these cultures.

Thousands of years ago people from Asia migrated to the Western Hemisphere and spread throughout the lands that would later be called North and South America. Over the millennia, before Europeans found their way there, these peoples settled the Western Hemisphere, and a number of elaborate Native cultures developed. The Aztec, Maya, and Inca had large cities in North, Central, and South America. In what is now the United States, Pueblo groups in the Southwest and the Mound Builders in the Mississippi River basin lived in large towns and small cities. People lived in every corner of the land and adapted to every climatic condition, from the frozen Arctic home of the Inuit to the hot, dry desert inhabited by the Tohono O'odham of what is now southern Arizona and northern Mexico.

When in A.D. 1492 Christopher Columbus arrived in what Europeans would call the Americas, he mistakenly thought he was in the part of Asia known as the Indies. Columbus therefore called the people he encountered Indians. These Native Americans all had their own names for their many tribes; however, as a group they are still often referred to as American Indians or just Indians. Each group of American Indians has its own story of how its ancestors were created and ended up in the group's traditional homelands. What is known about the Americas before the arrival of Europeans, however, has been determined mainly by studying the artifacts found at archaeological sites throughout the Americas. Despite the efforts of scientists from a wide variety of fields, there remain numerous questions about how these diverse cultures developed in North America. Scholars have a number of theories.

One part of the story that most people agree on is that present-day Native peoples of the Americas—including American Indians and Inuit—are descended from those who came to America from Asia. Many came on foot before the end of the last ice age, which ended about 10,000 years ago. Others, such as the Inuit, arrived much later as they spread out around the polar ice cap by boat and over the ice. Many sources refer to a "land bridge" that existed between what is now Siberia and Alaska and allowed the passage of people from Asia to North America. In many ways, this is a misleading term. During the last ice age, from about 40,000 years ago to 10,000 years ago, large sheets of ice called glaciers that were thousands of feet thick at times extended into North America as far as what is now the northern part of the United States. There was so much water locked into the glaciers that scientists estimate that the oceans were more than 400 feet lower than they are today.

The Bering Sea is the body of water that now lies between Siberia and Alaska. However, 400 feet beneath this sea is a land mass more than 1,000 miles wide. So, instead of talking about a

THE STUDY OF PALEO-INDIANS

Scientists from a variety of fields have worked to explain the origins of the more than 500 tribes that existed in North America at the end of the 15th century. The people who play the biggest role in this research are archaeologists. An archaeologist studies the past by finding objects called artifacts that people leave behind. Archaeologists refer to the earliest people in North America as Paleo-Indians. They use this term because they are studying people who lived during the Paleolithic period, or Old Stone Age, which existed from about 40,000 to 10,000 years ago in North America.

In addition to archaeologists digging up artifacts to study, other scientists contribute information about the plants, animals, climate, and geologic conditions that existed at the time. Still other scientists have developed numerous techniques to date the artifacts that the archaeologists dig up.

historical, narrow "land bridge" that facilitated the peopling of the Americas, it is important to see the area that scientists now refer to as Beringia as a wide, relatively flat plain that looked

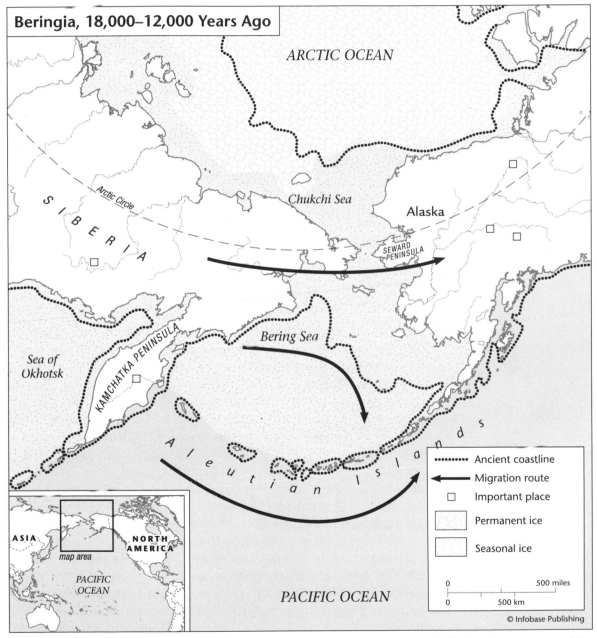

Beringia, 18,000–12,000 Years Ago

ARCTIC OCEAN

Arctic Circle

SIBERIA

Chukchi Sea

Alaska

SEWARD PENINSULA

Bering Sea

KAMCHATKA PENINSULA

Sea of Okhotsk

Aleutian Islands

ASIA

NORTH AMERICA

map area

PACIFIC OCEAN

PACIFIC OCEAN

·········· Ancient coastline

⟵ Migration route

☐ Important place

Permanent ice

Seasonal ice

0   500 miles

0   500 km

© Infobase Publishing

During the last ice age a wide plain between Asia and North America was exposed, allowing the ancestors of the American Indians to cross to the Americas. These first Americans traveled over land and across the seasonal sea ice that formed along the shoreline. Scientists refer to this area as Beringia, as it is now under the Bering Sea.

Glaciers, such as the one pictured here in the mountains of British Columbia, once covered most of the northern part of North America. *(Library of Congress, Prints and Photographs Division [LC-D4-14664])*

like the treeless tundra that still exists in the far north. Starting 25,000 years ago, or some would argue even earlier, bands of Paleolithic hunter-gatherers, people who lived by hunting animals and gathering wild plants, crossed Beringia, and the ice along its shores, to North America.

These first ancestors of the American Indians hunted many different animals that are now extinct. During this long ice age, many large mammals known as megafauna existed. They included mastodons, wooly mammoths, giant bison, and other large plant-eaters. There were also large predators such as American lions and saber-toothed tigers. The bones of many of these animals have been dug up at the campsites of Paleo-Indians.

Geologists, scientists who study the origins and changes in Earth's surface, believe that there was a period of time more than 23,000 years ago when people could have traveled down the Pacific coast. After that, the glaciers made it impossible for people to move south or to cross them. Then about 14,000 years ago, the coastal route was again open enough for migration. Approximately 11,500 years ago, the glacier in North America had melted to the point that there were two separate areas of ice. In the

West, much of the area from the mountains along the Pacific coast to the Rocky Mountains was covered by what is known as the Cordilleran ice sheet. In the East, ice covered the land in a continuous sheet from the Arctic Ocean south into what is today New England, New York, Ohio, Michigan, Wisconsin, Minnesota, and North and South Dakota. This is known as the Laurentide ice sheet. Between the two areas of glacier, there was an ice-free corridor from Alaska south into what is now the central plains of the United States. Many scientists agree that when this corridor opened, Paleo-Indians spread through the Americas.

Although most scientists agree on the major overland migration routes from Asia, some have suggested that Paleo-Indians may also have traveled down the Pacific coast of both North

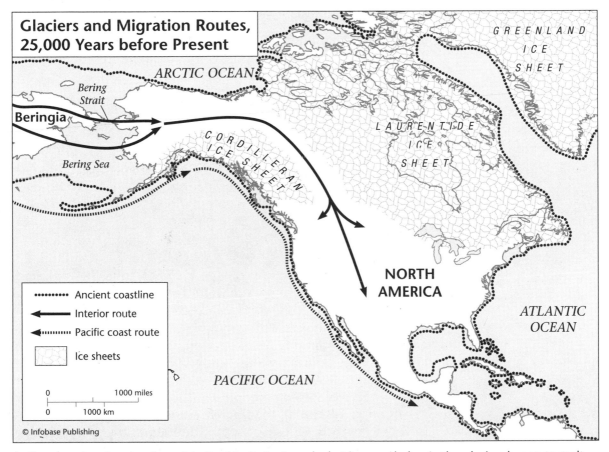

At first, people migrating from Asia lived in Beringia and what is now Alaska. As the glaciers began to melt, people were able to move south. The route along the Pacific coast opened up first, and then an ice-free area existed down through the North American plains.

and South America. They believe that boats may have been used by people who reached South America during these paleo-migrations. The fact that at least one site in southern Chile has been dated to at least 12,500 years ago would suggest that bands of people had spread out in the Americas well before the major migrations that appear to have taken place 11,500 years ago. The modern study of genetics has created speculation that one other possible route of migration existed during the Paleolithic period. Approximately 3 percent of American Indians share a genetic trait that is also found in parts of Europe. This has led to the idea that some people may have come from Europe by boat during Paleolithic times.

Most of what is believed about Paleo-Indians is very speculative because there are very few artifacts that have been found from these earliest Americans. It is now accepted, however, that as the glaciers receded, people spread through the Americas. They lived by hunting and gathering. It was once widely believed that these people lived primarily by hunting

Large animals known as megafauna, such as the wooly mammoth pictured here, roamed North America during the last ice age and were hunted by Paleo-Indians. *(© Science VU/Visuals Unlimited)*

STONE TOOLS

Although in some areas of North America the American Indians made tools and decorative objects out of copper and the Inuit were known to make knives out of iron from recovered meteorites, the vast majority of tools were made of stone. Knives used for cutting, points for spears and arrows, as well as small blades and scrapers used in a variety of tasks were all made by flaking off pieces of a variety of types of stones. Flint, chert, and obsidian are all types of rock that flake apart when struck.

To make stone tools, the toolmaker started with a large piece of rock and hit it with a rock hammer. Large flakes of stone would break off and then be broken into smaller usable shapes and sizes. To remove smaller and smaller pieces as the tool was shaped and sharpened, different methods were applied. Often the toolmaker would use the point of an antler to apply pressure to a specific spot on the stone to remove a flake. Sometimes the antler was struck with a piece of wood until a flake of stone was removed. Other toolmakers applied pressure to the antler tip until the flake came off. As the edge took shape, smaller and smaller pieces were removed until the edge was extremely sharp. If the edge became dull, it could be reworked to sharpen it. The sites where usable stone is found often show that they were mined by Native Americans for thousands of years, going back to Paleo-Indian times.

large animals such as the wooly mammoth and the giant bison. Although there are many archaeological sites that contain the bones of these large animals, it is now thought that these people also hunted many smaller animals and gathered the edible parts of many wild plants.

The original weapons of these early American Indians consisted of wooden spears with tips that had been hardened with fire. Some time after people were able to use the migration route in the center of North America, they began to attach stone points onto their spears. It is by the size and style of these stone points that archaeologists have been able to identify and group people into a number of paleocultural groups.

As archaeologists discovered early sites of human occupation in North America, they noticed that different groups used different shaped tools. These groups were usually named after the location of the sites where their artifacts were first found. Three of these earliest groups were first discovered in New Mexico, and one was found in Texas. Evidence of the New Mexico groups was first found near the towns of Clovis and Folsom, and the third group was found in the Sandia Mountains east of Albuquerque. The fourth group was first discovered near Plainview,

Clovis-style stone spear points are found in many locations throughout North America, indicating a relationship between early hunter-gatherer groups. *(Photo courtesy of Pete Bostrom)*

Texas, and is referred to as the Plano culture. Each of these groups had its own unique style of making their stone spear points; therefore, archaeologists can easily identify a Clovis- or Folsom-style spear point wherever it is found.

As the glaciers continued to recede, the people of these groups spread out in search of animals to hunt and plants to gather. Clovis-style spear points have been found throughout much of North America, and at one time scientists believed the Clovis people were the first North Americans. It is now known that the earliest Clovis sites date to about 11,500 years ago and that people were in the Americas long before that. Some people suggest that the Clovis people were a new wave of migration into the Americas. Others think that they had been in Alaska for a long time and moved south about this time as travel became possible down the center of North America. It may never be known which theories are accurate.

What is known for certain is that these early culture groups in the center of the continent spread east, west, and south. It is also known that the climate began to change. Between 10,000 and 5,000 B.C., North America went from the Ice Age with its large Pleistocene (time period from 1.6 million to 10,000 years ago) animals, like the saber-toothed tiger and wooly mammoth, to the climate and landscape that exists today. The Paleo-Indians that existed at the beginning of this time learned from generation to generation to adapt to changes in their environment.

Over thousands of years between the end of the last ice age and the coming of Europeans to North America, the different cultures of American Indians developed along a number of lines. As the climate became less severe, American Indians spread out to cover the entire continent. They created new technologies to deal with the vastly different environments that they encountered. By the end of this time, the American Indians had broken into distinct language groups and eventually into a wide variety of tribes.

Modern researchers divided North America, excluding Mexico, into 10 cultural regions, known as culture areas, to aid in their study of American Indians. In classifying these areas, scientists took many factors into account. Among those were similarity in culture, environment, and geography. Within a culture area there may be a number of tribes that speak languages that differ, however, the way they have adapted to the geography of the region gave groups many similarities. For example, in the California Culture Area almost all groups used acorns as a major source of food. Therefore, they all had similar technology for harvesting, processing, cooking, and preserving acorns. In the Plateau Culture Area the prolific runs of salmon in the many rivers of the region became the primary food source and focus of the culture. Each of the ten regions has similar unifying aspects.

In some of these culture areas, however, there are numerous distinctions that can be made between groups in the region. For instance, in the Southwest, two distinct cultures live side by side within one culture area. One group known as Pueblo Indians (*pueblo* is the Spanish word for "town") lived in towns and were primarily farmers: Others consisted of various groups, such as

Acoma Pueblo in New Mexico is the oldest continuously inhabited community in the United States. Pueblo people have lived in Acoma for more than 1,000 years. *(Library of Congress, Prints and Photographs Division [LC-USZ62-74105])*

During World War II, the U.S. Army recruited members of the Navajo (Dineh) tribe to create a code using Navajo to transmit sensitive messages. This code proved indecipherable to enemies. *(Official U.S. Marine Corps photo USMC #69896/National Archives and Records Administration)*

the related Navajo (Dineh) and Apache, who were seminomadic and depended much more on hunting and gathering than on agriculture. In this region, the unifying aspect is more closely related to geography and climate of the region.

The culture areas that most scientists agree on are the Northeast, Southeast, Great Plains, Great Basin, Plateau, Southwest, California, Northwest Coast, Subarctic, and Arctic. Each volume in this series will show how the peoples in a culture area developed their distinct way of life, making the transition from Ice Age hunters/gatherers to the complex tribal cultures that existed when Christopher Columbus landed in the Caribbean in 1492. The lifeways and material culture of these people will be described in depth. Spiritual beliefs and social structure are also explained. Furthermore, readers will learn of the wide variety of housing and transportation developed for each region. Clothing and everyday items will be described, as will hunting, fishing, farming, and cooking practices. Readers will also learn how the American Indians fought to survive the long invasion of European settlers that followed Columbus and explore how, despite the best attempts of Europeans to eliminate the American Indians almost everywhere they found them, many tribes persevered and continue to exist today.

The long and fascinating history of Indian peoples is described, illuminating the many contributions made by Indians and Indian cultures to the broader American culture. In the 20th century, Indians finally began to have some success in regaining some land and respect. Indian soldiers fought bravely in various wars the United States participated in. All American Indians finally gained citizenship. Protests starting in the 1950s and 1960s as well as the work of Indian leaders resulted in victories in the courts and legislative chambers of North America. Increased pride in their heritage and a resurgence of Indian cultures have given many American Indians an optimistic outlook for the future as the 21st century unfolds.

Stone Age Hunters to Riverine Culture on the Plateau

The Plateau Culture Area is the vast area encompassing all or part of the modern-day states of Washington, Oregon, Idaho, Montana, and California, as well as the Canadian province of British Columbia. The Plateau region is surrounded by mountains: The Rocky Mountains are its eastern boundary while the Cascade Range separates the area from the Northwest coast. Two major river systems flow through the area. The Columbia River and its many tributaries drain the southern plateau while the Fraser River system is the primary feature to the north. The two river systems played a major role in the development of Plateau Indian culture.

When discussing the prehistory of the region, scientists usually divide the Plateau into three subregions. The divisions are based in part on differences in the environment and in part because the Plateau spans two countries. The Northern Plateau is generally considered the area that falls north of the U.S.-Canadian border and is sometimes referred to as the Canadian Plateau. This area includes the entire Fraser River drainage and the northernmost reaches of the Columbia River tributaries.

The Southern Plateau is south of the U.S.-Canadian border and includes the area drained by the middle section of the Columbia River and all its tributaries up to where the migration of fish from the ocean is blocked by natural barriers such as waterfalls. The Southern Plateau is less forested and has less variation in elevation than the Northern Plateau. Much of this area is a rolling plain with a high desert climate.

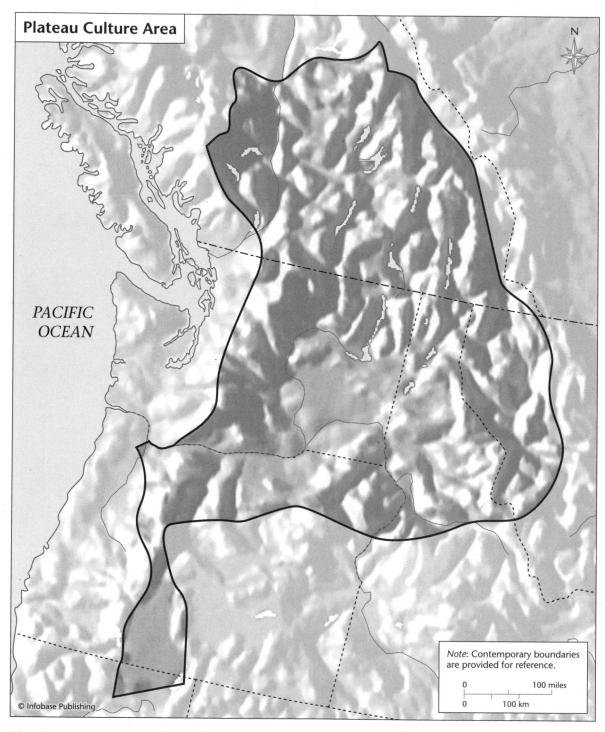

Plateau Culture Area

PACIFIC
OCEAN

Note: Contemporary boundaries
are provided for reference.

0   100 miles

0   100 km

© Infobase Publishing

The Plateau Culture Area includes the territories of the northwestern United States (excluding Alaska),
California, and British Columbia, Canada, that are bounded by the Rocky Mountains and the coastal
Cascade Range, which is drained by the Thompson and Columbia Rivers.

The Columbia River, which flows through the middle section of the Plateau Culture Area, has many natural waterfalls, including Kettle Falls (pictured here) in northeastern Washington State. *(National Archives and Records Administration)*

The final division is the area to the east of the Columbia plateau that drains into the Columbia but does not have migrations of salmon and steelhead trout from the ocean. This Eastern Plateau is in northern Idaho and northwestern Montana.

In addition to the geographical divisions, the prehistory of the area is divided into three time periods that date back to 9000 B.C. The early period runs from about 9000 to 6000 B.C. This is followed by a middle period from about 6000 to 2000 B.C. The third division of the Plateau's prehistory is referred to as the late period and is given the time range of 2000 B.C. to A.D. 1720. In its more than 10,000 years of prehistory, the Plateau went through a number of climactic changes that affected the American Indian culture of the area. Throughout the prehistory and history of the region, the rivers have been very important to the people who lived there.

EARLY PERIOD
(9000 to 6000 B.C.)
During the early period, the people of the Plateau lived together in small nomadic bands and wandered the region hunting and gathering food. At this time, the climate of the

The Marmes Rockshelter in southeast Washington State may be one of the oldest dwellings in the Plateau Culture Area. Bones and tools found in the Marmes Rockshelter have aided archaeologists in learning more about the early inhabitants of the Plateau Culture Area. *(Washington State University)*

SCIENCE HELPS ARCHAEOLOGISTS

Scientists use a number of methods to determine the age of an archaeological site. One of the most often used is the carbon-14 method. All living organisms have a known amount of carbon-14 molecules. When an organism dies, carbon-14 molecules begin to disintegrate at a standard rate. By measuring the amount of carbon-14 in a piece of wood uncovered at an archaeological site, scientists can tell when that wood was cut from a living tree. Although conditions of the material and the site can cause a certain amount of error, carbon-14 dating is very important in determining the age of a site.

Scientists use other methods as well. The depth and number of layers of sediment at a site can help a geologist determine how long ago an artifact was left at a site. This method is called geochronology. To date more recent sites, scientists have developed a time line based on the pattern created by the growth rings of certain types of trees. This is referred to as dendrochronology. By overlapping a large number of samples, they have been able to extend the dendrochronological time line back almost 4,000 years. Scientists can also tell when an obsidian stone tool was made by measuring the amount of moisture that has escaped from the stone. This is known as obsidian hydration dating.

In addition to dating objects, scientists can also determine certain aspects of a person's diet by examining the stable carbon isotope in their bones. A stable carbon isotope is a carbon molecule that has completed its process of decay. This method has been especially helpful in studying Plateau culture because it allows scientists to determine how much of a person's diet had been made up of marine protein. This helped people determine that the Indians of the area became more and more dependent on the annual salmon and steelhead runs in the nearby rivers.

region was even drier than it is today, forcing people to stay close to the rivers for a reliable source of water. As it is today, the rivers of the area ran year-round, bringing water from the eastern slope of the Cascades and the western side of the Rocky Mountains. The earliest evidence of people living in the Plateau region has been found along the rivers, often in natural caves.

One of the most important early sites is known as the Marmes Rockshelter in southeast Washington on the banks of the lower Snake River. As archaeologists excavated the layers of sediment and debris that filled the cave during the thousands of years since their use, they have learned much about the earliest inhabitants of the Plateau. The first inhabitants of the rockshelter left behind the bones of many animals and fishes they had eaten as well as numerous stone tools. As the size and shape of the stone tools changed over time, archaeologists can

Art, such as petroglyphs, or rock paintings or sculpture, provide clues about early inhabitants of areas. The petroglyph face of Tsagiglalal, "She Who Watches," is painted near The Dalles, Oregon, near the Columbia River. *(Library of Congress, Prints and Photographs Division [LC-USZ62-49642])*

use these different types of tools to date other sites by the style of the stone tools found there.

In the beginning of human habitation in the Plateau region, the rivers of the area still carried large amounts of silt (fine particles of dirt) and tended to get too warm in the summer for ocean fish to migrate up them to spawn. However, on the lower sections of the rivers, the water could support the fish. Sites in that area indicate that people had begun to take advantage of this easily harvested source of food. One such site on the Columbia River is known as Fivemile Rapids, near the present-day town of The Dalles, Oregon. At Fivemile Rapids, archaeologists have found more than 150,000 salmon skeletons dating to a time in the early period of the Plateau's prehistory.

MIDDLE PERIOD
(6000 to 2000 B.C.)
The middle period of the Plateau's prehistory was a time of transition. During this time, the climate began to cool and became more like it is today. As this happened, the water in the rivers remained cooler during the summers. At the same time, the rivers had cleared themselves of much of the silt that had been a result of glacial deposits in the valleys from the last ice age. These changes made it possible for the migration of salmon and steelhead to spread farther and farther upstream. As the fish expanded their territory, the number of fish that entered the rivers from the Pacific Ocean also increased.

In this photograph, a white-tailed jackrabbit stands still in the snow. The meat and the hides of animals such as rabbits were an important resource for people of the Plateau Culture Area. (U.S. Fish and Wildlife Service)

As the Indians of the Plateau were able to harvest more and more fish, they learned ways of preserving fish for use in the winter. This allowed settlement along the rivers in semi-permanent villages, especially between 3300 and 2000 B.C. In addition to river villages, people moved seasonally to harvest game and plants that were available for food. In addition to fish, the people of the Plateau took advantage of a number of other food sources. Archaeological sites from this period indicate that freshwater mussels were collected by many groups. They also hunted extensively in the months when the fish were not running.

The hunters of the Plateau harvested a wide variety of game. Two of the most important for both food and hides were deer and rabbits. A number of wild plants were also harvested for food during this time period. Roots were extremely important and would remain so well into the historic period. A wide variety of nuts and berries were harvested. Nuts from pine trees were gathered and required people to move away from the rivers into the pine forests at higher elevations. Despite the importance of these other foods in the diet of the people of the Plateau, scientists have determined, using the stable carbon isotope method, that the protein in some diets consisted of 40 percent fish. The percentage of fish eaten rose through the end of the middle period and into the late period.

The middle period also saw a change in housing. As people were able to spend more and more of the year in one place, they

PLATEAU AGRICULTURE

Many American Indians learned how to grow corn and other crops during this middle period. The first corn had been grown in central Mexico around 8000 B.C. and then spread north and south. The Indians of the Southwest, Southeast, Northeast, and the Plains (before the introduction of the horse) came to depend on agriculture to supply a large percentage of their food. In the Plateau region, people never adopted the agricultural methods understood today. However, they learned how to improve the yield of numerous wild plants by weeding out competing species, pruning plants, and burning areas to encourage desirable plants. This form of agriculture was very effective in maintaining adequate supplies of the roots and other plants they gathered.

Trade among the people of the Plateau Culture Area revolved around such items as shells and animal skins. In this 1910 portrait by Edward S. Curtis, a Cayuse woman wears a necklace and earrings made from shells. *(Library of Congress, Prints and Photographs Division [LC-USZ62-109716])*

began to build permanent structures. The most common type of housing structure in the Plateau region in prehistoric times is called a pithouse. Pithouses of the middle period tended to be oval and ranged in size from nine feet in diameter to 40 feet.

The floor of these houses was below the level of the surrounding ground and had a pole frame that supported a roof and walls made of woven mats.

During the middle period, trade also became important in the Plateau region. The primary trade routes were up and down rivers. Jewelry fashioned from a variety of seashells is often found at sites far upriver. In addition, archaeologists have found stone pipes and beads made from stone from outside the area. There seems to have been a small amount of trade with other regions as well. Some trade existed with the people of the Great Basin to the south, the Subarctic to the north, and even through the passes of the Rocky Mountains to the Plains. As time went on, the people of the Plateau participated in more and more trade within their own region and with surrounding cultural areas.

LATE PERIOD
(2000 B.C. to A.D. 1720)

Change came slowly to the prehistoric culture of the Plateau. At the beginning of this period, the climate of the Plateau continued to cool. This allowed for the forests of the region to spread to lower elevations on the sides of the mountains. Cooling also meant an increase in high-elevation glaciers and more snow for longer periods in mountains not high enough to form glaciers. This change in the climate had two effects on the waters of the Plateau rivers. First, it reduced the summer water temperature, and second, it maintained a higher flow of water throughout the summer and fall. The changes in the rivers served to greatly increase the number of sea-run fish that swam upstream each year.

The increase in fish allowed for a corresponding growth in population and in individual settlements. On the lower reaches of the large rivers of the Plateau, villages of more than 100 houses became common by the middle of the late prehistoric period. Skeletal remains from this time show an increase in fish consumption. More than half the diet of many Plateau Indians came from marine sources. People also continued to hunt and gather for additional food. A larger variety of roots became important staples in the diet of the Plateau. Large storage pits and special ovens to cook roots have been found in archaeological sites dating from this period.

The increase in population on the Plateau also seems to have caused some conflict between groups. Some villages from this time were built on islands where people were safer from attack. Also, there are remains of fortified campsites on the tops

GLACIERS FEED THE PLATEAU

As the climate cooled 3,000 years ago, the number and extent of the glaciers in the mountains surrounding the Plateau increased. The melting of the snowpack in the mountains in the spring and the continued melting of the glaciers each summer and fall were a reliable source of water for the arid valleys of the Plateau. During more than 400 years ending around A.D. 1850, the glaciers of the area reached their largest size since the last ice age. Some geologists even refer to this period as the Little Ice Age.

Today, there are still many glaciers on the highest peaks of the region. In Glacier National Park in northwestern Montana, there are 50 separate glaciers. On Mount Rainier, the highest peak in Washington, glaciers cover 36 square miles above the mountain's tree line. The Carbon Glacier on Mount Rainier is 700 feet thick—the thickest in the United States—and comes to the lowest elevation of any glacier in the lower 48 states.

The tops of most of the mountains of the coastal range in British Columbia are covered by extensive glaciers, many of which drain into the Fraser River watershed. In addition, there are numerous glaciers in the Canadian Rocky Mountains.

Since 1850, the glaciers surrounding the Plateau region have shrunk and grown with slight variations in the climate. However, starting in the last quarter of the 20th century, many glaciers in North America have shown a large decrease in both their size and volume. The Sierra Club reports that of the 150 glaciers that existed in Glacier National Park in 1850 only 50 remain today. Some scientists blame a general warming trend. However, many believe that global warming is being increased by gases released into the atmosphere by vehicles, power plants, and other types of equipment that use gas and oil for fuels. Some predict that within approximately 25 years, most of the glaciers in the United States, excluding Alaska, will be gone.

Glacier National Park, in northwestern Montana, is notable for its dense forests and lush valleys. The terrain of the park resembles the habitat of the first inhabitants of the Plateau Culture Area. *(National Park Service)*

of mesas in the areas where people journeyed to collect roots and to hunt. Despite the apparent increase in conflict between Plateau tribes, trade continued to be an important activity.

In addition to trading for decorative goods like shells for jewelry, there was also an exchange in technology. The use of the bow and arrow appeared in the Plateau area around 400 B.C. and by A.D. 500 was the most common weapon for hunting and warfare throughout the region. The most common flow of trade was with the coastal tribes up and down both the Columbia and Fraser River systems.

By A.D. 1000, the people of the Plateau had divided into the tribes that existed at the beginning of contact with non-Native technology and people. Scholars mark the beginning of the historical period with the arrival of the first horses in the Plateau region around 1720. The grass plains of the Plateau were ideal for raising horses. The people of the Plateau quickly became some of the most accomplished horse riders and breeders among the American Indians. The increased mobility that horses provided caused substantial changes to Plateau culture.

The first horses arrived on the Plateau from other Indian groups in the south, where the horse had been introduced by the Spanish. The horse was well established on the Plateau before the arrival of the first non-Indians. In addition, European disease arrived on the Plateau before European people. Some have suggested that the first outbreak of smallpox in the Plateau region probably took place in the late 1600s. It is believed that it was transmitted from coastal tribes who had been infected by Europeans sailing along the northwest coast trading for furs. Despite the effects of European contact, most parts of the Plateau remained unknown to non-Indians until the early years of the 19th century.

2

The Cycles of Life

⚊ FAMILY ORGANIZATION

The most important societal unit among the Indians of the Plateau was the family. Many Plateau communities were made up of extended families that cooperated in hunting, fishing, and gathering activities. The family's first responsibility was to provide the basic necessities for its members. Older members of the family, grandparents and older aunts and uncles, were treated with respect and were provided for by the families of their sons and sometimes their daughters. From birth through death, the family took care of its members.

When a woman was pregnant, she would observe certain taboos. Although these varied somewhat from tribe to tribe in the Plateau region, pregnant women avoided certain foods. They also avoided looking at certain objects, such as dead animals, that might frighten the baby. Expectant mothers often strenuously exercised, including running and swimming. Although some groups valued twins, other tribes tried to avoid them. They believed that if a woman always slept on her side she could prevent the formation of twins.

When a woman went into labor, she would move to a special birthing hut where she would be away from the rest of the community. One or more older women would join her in the birthing hut. These women would act as midwives and assist the woman in the delivery of her baby. In some instances, the woman's husband would also be in the birthing hut.

If there were problems with the delivery, a shaman, who was both religious leader and doctor for the community, would be

Children of the Plateau Culture Area would spend their first few months of life attached to a cradleboard. In this 1910 photograph by Edward S. Curtis, a Cayuse mother poses with her child, who rests in a cradleboard. *(Library of Congress, Prints and Photographs Division [LC-USZ62-89974])*

summoned to help. Some groups had women shamans who were specialists in aiding in childbirth. The shaman would use a combination of herbal remedies, physical manipulation of the fetus in the womb, and special prayers to help with the delivery. When the baby was born, the umbilical cord would be tied off with a stringlike sinew from a deer. One of the midwives would then bite the cord to separate the baby from the placenta. When the cord later dried and fell off, it would be placed in a small leather pouch so it could be saved.

The mother and baby would stay in the birthing hut up to five days. During this time, a relative who was the same gender as the baby would prepare a cradleboard for the new member of the family. The pouch with the umbilical cord would be attached to the cradleboard. Babies would spend much of their time attached to their cradleboards during the first months of their lives. Among many of the tribes in the southern Plateau region, a pad was placed on the baby's forehead and then bound snugly to the cradleboard. This caused the baby's forehead to slope back more than it would naturally. It also caused the head to come to more of a point. Although this practice ended soon after non-Indians moved into the Plateau in the early part of the 19th century, some historians have suggested that the Flathead tribe got their name because they did not practice binding the heads of their babies.

Small children were often the responsibility of older children in their family group. As children grew, they were often cared for by grandparents and older aunts and uncles. Often their parents and others of their parents' generation were involved in gathering, preserving, and preparing food for the survival of the whole family. As children grew, they started to learn the gender-specific skills they would need to help their family. Boys would spend more and more time with their uncles and grandfathers, learning hunting and fishing skills. Girls learned how to preserve and prepare food, as well as how to make clothing and other household items.

Sharing was an important aspect of life for the people of the Plateau. No one person could survive on his or her own; cooperation was a way of life. To ingrain this idea in young people, the first time a boy killed an animal or caught some fish or a young girl collected berries or roots, that food was always given away to other members of the family in a ceremonial meal.

Children were often given a number of names as they were growing up. These names were generally based on some event or characteristic of the child. When children were approximately nine, they received their official name. It was usually the name of an ancestor who was well remembered. Most of the time, the naming ceremony involved a feast put on by the child's family and the giving of gifts. However, the gifts were for the people invited to the feast and not for the child.

The lives of all members of the group were closely connected to the spirit world they perceived around them. Both boys and girls in most groups were encouraged to seek a vision to find a special spirit to guide them in life.

Preparation for a vision quest involved strenuous exercise, fasting, sweat baths, and immersion in cold river water. Some groups also had the young people seeking visions drink herbal brews that

Among the tribes of the Plateau Culture Area, men and women were assigned very different tasks. Innocence, an Umatilla, leans against a tree in this 1910 portrait by Edward S. Curtis. *(Library of Congress, Prints and Photographs Division [LC-USZ62-110503])*

THE SWEAT LODGE

The sweat lodge and the sweat baths that people took in them remain important aspects of the spiritual life of many American Indians in the Plateau region and throughout North America. The Plateau sweat lodges were of two basic types—earth-covered lodges and temporary lodges made with a pole frame and covered with brush, mats, or hides. Both types of sweat lodges worked in the same way. Rocks were heated in a fire and then placed in the lodge. Water was then poured on the rocks, creating steam. As the temperature and steam rose in the sweat lodge, those inside would sweat profusely. Plateau Indians believed that sweating purified the body, and the sweat lodge was often used prior to religious ceremonies, hunts, and even warfare.

Sweat lodges provided a way for people of the Plateau Culture Area to cleanse themselves before spiritual ceremonies and other activities. A sweat lodge is situated against a backdrop of hills and rocky terrain in this 1910 photograph by Edward S. Curtis. *(Library of Congress, Prints and Photographs Division [LC-USZ62-111290])*

were intended to purge their systems. Often boys were sent off into the mountains for one or more nights to help them make contact with their individual spirit. The spirit was usually that of an animal that taught the young person a special spirit song.

The type of spirit that came to a person often indicated something about the person's future. Some spirits were believed to help make good hunters or fishermen, while another spirit might indicate a person would be a successful gambler.

By the time boys and girls reached puberty, they were ready to take on their roles as unmarried adults. Boys took a full role in hunting and fishing activities while young women worked with their mothers and other female relatives to help with all the domestic duties that fell to the women of the group. Marriage usually took place when both young men and women reached their midteens.

Marriage was an important point in the life of the young people of the Plateau. Arrangements for marriage varied somewhat from tribe to tribe. Among the people of most tribes, there were a variety of ways that a young man and woman agreed to get married. Some marriages were arranged by the parents of the intended couple; however, either one could refuse to marry. Other marriages came about because of a proposal by either the man or woman.

Traditional marriage ceremonies among people of the Plateau Culture Area consisted of numerous feasts and dances. A Wishram bride wears a ceremonial wedding outfit including a beaded headdress, dentalium shell earrings, beaded necklace, and a beaded buckskin dress in this 1910 portrait by Edward S. Curtis. *(Library of Congress, Prints and Photographs Division [LC USZ62-105387])*

Sometimes villages would hold a ceremonial dance for all the single young people who were old enough to get married. During this dance, a young man would take hold of a sash worn by a woman he wanted to marry. If she allowed him to hold onto the sash it was considered her agreement to an engagement. After the dance, the two families would meet to agree upon the marriage. Once a marriage was arranged, there would be an exchange of gifts and feasts between the families and friends of the bride and groom.

Unlike the accepted practices today, the gifts were not for the bride and groom but for guests at the wedding feasts. Usually the groom's family gave the first feast, during which they would give away more gifts than the bride's family. After the bride's family's feast, the couple were considered married. The newly married couple would often move in with the bride's family for a period of time. Often they would remain with the bride's family until their first child was born. At that time, the most common practice was for a married couple to join the husband's family, either moving in with his parents or creating their own dwelling nearby.

The husband and wife became an important team in the subsistence of their family. The man was expected to hunt and fish to provide food. The woman was responsible for preserving and preparing food, making clothes, and gathering roots, berries, and other useful plant food. A couple was part of their extended family and depended on the cooperation of their larger family for many tasks. An older member of the family was usually considered the head of the family, and this role usually fell to a man.

The people of the Plateau were taught from a very early age that cooperation was important to their survival, and they viewed their elders with respect. This respect can be seen in their funeral practices. When a person died, the community and especially their family wanted to ensure that the spirit of the person who had died would have an easy journey to the afterlife. Among some of the Plateau tribes, a four- to five-day wake was held to allow the deceased's spirit time to pass to the afterlife. During this time, the body would be arranged in the dead person's home and his or her relatives would keep vigil around the body.

After the wake, the body was buried. There were no formal cemeteries among the Plateau people, and bodies were often buried among the rocks that accumulate at the bottom of steep slopes. People were buried in their best clothes, often with a number of personal possessions. After a body was buried, the person's remaining belongings were given away. The husband or wife of the deceased would remain in mourning for an extended period of time. Both men and women of the Plateau wore their hair in long braids. As a sign of mourning, both men and women would often cut their braids off and mourning would continue until their hair grew back out.

TRIBAL ORGANIZATION

Among the people of the Plateau, the first loyalty was to their immediate and extended families. Next in importance was their village, which was often made up of a number of related families. Within the family, a highly regarded elder was usually considered the family leader. At the village level, there was usually one leader who either by accomplishment or heredity oversaw the daily events of the community. This person was usually a male and often served as an arbiter in disputes among the people of the village.

In addition to the village leader, other leaders were appointed for a variety of communal tasks. These would include fishing, hunting, gathering, and warfare. For their hunting, fishing, and gathering activities, the leaders would be older men or women who were respected for their knowledge and skill in a given activity. For example, the hunting leader would decide when and where the group would travel to hunt and would organize and assign members of the group to the various activities that were needed for a successful hunt. A war leader would be someone who could enlist warriors to follow him. Prior to the coming of non-Indians and firearms, warfare on the Plateau was usually small in scale and consisted of raids on villages or groups from other tribes. A warrior who had been successful in previous raids found it easy to recruit followers for other raids.

Once horses and then firearms arrived in the Plateau region, warfare changed dramatically. Warriors and hunters traveling by horse could cover much more ter-

Prior to the introduction of firearms, warfare among the tribes of the Plateau Culture Area was mainly small in scale. Yellow Wolf of the Nez Perce tribe poses for a 1909 portrait while holding a tomahawk and rifle. *(Library of Congress, Prints and Photographs Division [LC-USZ62-122130])*

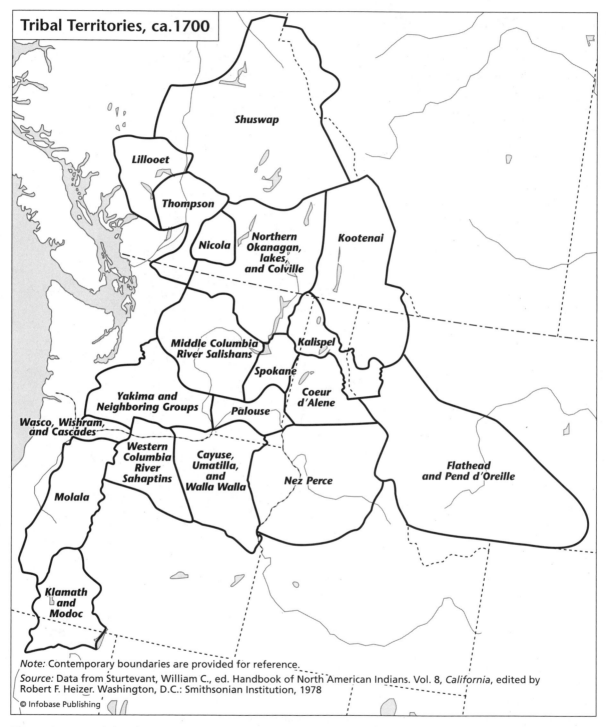

Tribal Territories, ca.1700

Shuswap

Lillooet

Thompson

Nicola

Northern
Okanagan,
lakes,
and Colville

Kootenai

Middle Columbia
River Salishans

Kalispel

Spokane

Coeur
d'Alene

Yakima and
Neighboring Groups

Palouse

Wasco, Wishram,
and Cascades

Western
Columbia
River
Sahaptins

Cayuse,
Umatilla,
and
Walla Walla

Nez Perce

Flathead
and Pend d'Oreille

Molala

Klamath
and
Modoc

Note: Contemporary boundaries are provided for reference.

Source: Data from Sturtevant, William C., ed. Handbook of North American Indians. Vol. 8, *California*, edited by Robert F. Heizer. Washington, D.C.: Smithsonian Institution, 1978

© Infobase Publishing

The entire area of the Plateau was used by the American Indians of the region until they were forced to move onto the restricted space of a few reservations.

LANGUAGES OF THE PLATEAU

Among the many tribes of the Plateau, most of the languages spoken came from two language families. Penutian and Salish. In addition, the Kootenai spoke a language that appears to be unique in the area.

PENUTIAN LANGUAGES
Cayuse
Klamath
Klickitat
Modoc
Nez Perce
Palouse
Umatilla
Walla Walla
Yakama

SALISH LANGUAGES
Coeur d'Alene
Colville
Kalispel
Salish-Kootenai (Flathead)
Sanpoil
Spokane

KOOTENAI LANGUAGE
Kootenai

ritory, and the herds of horses belonging to opposing tribes were common targets of raids. Plateau hunters also began traveling to the Plains region to hunt buffalo. Here they came into conflict with the Plains tribes who considered this an invasion of their territory. In the 19th century, many Plateau tribes would become involved in major conflicts with non-Indians who moved in and took over their territory.

The vast lands of the Plateau were largely uninhabited, but the numerous tribes of the area traveled great distances within their own territories on a seasonal basis. For this reason, each village and tribe claimed a large traditional territory. Some families, through tradition and intermarriage, were able to hunt, fish, and gather food beyond the limits of their community or tribe's lands. Each tribe consisted of groups of people who spoke the same language, and there were a number of languages and tribes in the Plateau region.

In addition to the village and task leaders, each Plateau community had one or more religious leaders. These people are referred to as shamans. A shaman was part priest, part doctor, and part historian. The shaman would often lead various religious ceremonies throughout the year. They would function as the community's doctors. Their approach to caring for a sick or injured person was multileveled. They had an extensive knowledge of the medicinal properties of numerous plants that they gave to their patients. They also knew how to set bones and, as in the case of delivering babies, how to manipulate the body like a modern-day chiropractor. A belief was also widely held that disease involved something the sick person had done to anger the spirit world. To counteract this, the shaman served as an intermediary between the sick person and the spirit world.

3

Houses, Clothing, Tools, and Transportation

HOUSES

Most people of the Plateau had three basic needs for shelter. During the winter, they needed a large shelter that would house a large number of people and protect them from the cold weather. They also had semipermanent shelters at seasonal hunting, fishing, and gathering sites. In addition, they created temporary shelters when traveling or on resource collecting trips of relatively short duration.

The most substantial and widespread type of dwelling in the Plateau region was the pithouse, a semi-subterranean longhouse. The size and shape of pithouses varied among the different tribes and depended on the number of people who lived in them. Construction was similar among most groups. The first step was to dig a pit from two to six feet deep. This pit would reflect the size of the finished dwelling. Smaller houses for one or two nuclear families might be circular and measure only 20 feet in diameter. Bigger houses, however, were more common, and the largest were 20 or more feet wide and up to 100 feet long.

Once the pit was dug, it was often lined with rocks to make the walls. A frame of wooden posts was then erected to support the roof. The roof was covered with a variety of materials depending on their availability. Hand-hewn wooden planks were a common building material used by the Indians of the northwestern coastal area. These materials were adopted by some Plateau tribes that lived on the lower reaches of the Columbia and Fraser Rivers and had contact with coastal tribes. Other groups used bark or

TULE REEDS

An important resource for the people of the Plateau was the tall tule reeds that grew in the many lakes and quiet stretches of the region's rivers. Tule is a type of bulrush that regularly grows from three to nine feet in height. Each plant consists of a long smooth stalk topped by a cluster of small flower spikes.

The stalks of the tule were used in many ways. One of their most important uses was to create mats to cover their building structures. These mats were also hung on walls and used as dividers in multifamily dwellings and used to cover the dirt floors of Plateau houses. In addition to being made into mats, tule reeds were used to make a number of other useful objects. Sandals, leggings, skirts, baskets, and fish traps were just some objects made wholly from tule reeds.

In the Plateau Culture Area, tipis were typically constructed with tule, a type of bulrush. Edna Kash-kash of northern Oregon sits in front of a tipi in this photograph by Lee Moorhouse, ca. 1900. *(Library of Congress, Prints and Photographs Division [LC-USZ62-102133])*

tule mats to cover the roof. Often, the dirt that had been dug out of the pit was piled against the lower part of the roof to help insulate the dwelling from the cold.

In the larger houses, the interior was divided into compartments down each side with one nuclear family living in each compartment. In the center of the structure, extra space was created for use as a passageway and as a place for the winter hearths. Each family had its own hearth and a slot was left in the center of the roof to allow the smoke from the fires to escape and light to enter the house. For entrance, a wooden ladder was placed at one end of the house. If a village was along a river, the houses were built so they ran parallel to the water. Up to 100 people would live together in a large pithouse that might extend to 60 feet across.

In addition to their winter houses, people also built a variety of summer houses. Some groups built cone-shaped pole frames that they covered with mats or bark. Other groups built lean-tos (simple sloped frames) that were often set close together, facing each other, that would be occupied by related families. Sometimes the lean-tos were made very long to mirror the design of the winter longhouses. This type of shelter would be built at a fishing camp and it would be used year after year.

After interacting with tribes from the Great Plains, many tribes of the Plateau Culture Area adopted the tipi for temporary housing. A Yakama mat lodge is situated in a grassy field in Washington State in this 1910 photograph by Edward S. Curtis. *(Library of Congress, Prints and Photographs Division [LC-USZ62-99798])*

The third type of structure common in the Plateau region was temporary shelters. These consisted of a frame covered with mats, bark, or brush. Often the material for the frames was gathered locally while the mats might be transported from the main village. When the Plateau tribes acquired horses and began traveling over the mountains to the Plains to hunt buffalo, they adopted the Plains-style tipi covered with buffalo hides.

Traditional clothing of people of the Plateau Culture Area consisted of items made from such animals as deer, birds, and rabbits. Yellow Bird of the Umatilla tribe models traditional clothing in front of a backdrop while holding a tomahawk in this portrait ca. 1871–1907. *(National Archives and Records Administration)*

CLOTHING

There were two distinct clothing styles worn by the people of the Plateau. It appears that the more traditional material for clothing was woven from a variety of fibers. These included leggings, skirts, and moccasins woven from tule reeds as well as shirts, skirts, and aprons woven from fibers from other plants. As time went on and there was more contact with the Indians of the Plains, there is evidence that Plateau Indians wore more and more clothing made of the tanned deer hide often referred to as buckskin.

There was also a difference in the winter and summer outfits. In the summer, men wore a breech-cloth consisting of a single sheet of buckskin that went between the legs and was held up by a belt. Often this was all that was worn during warm weather. As temperatures dropped, a shirt, leggings, and moccasins were added to the outfit. Women wore long dresses, short leggings, and moccasins year-round. Many people had shirts that were decorated with fringe, painted designs, and a variety of shells and other animal parts such as porcupine quills.

In the coldest time of the year, men and women added a robe to their outfits. Many of these robes were made from the skins of animals with thick fur like the buffalo or beaver. Others wore robes that were woven from strips of bird skin that still had the insulating feathers attached. One common form of robe was made by sewing together many narrow strips of rabbit fur. Rabbits were plentiful in the Plateau region and were often hunted.

Both men and women wore hats. The type of hat varied throughout the region. Many groups wore hats that were woven like baskets with intricate patterns achieved by using differently dyed fibers. Some groups wore fur hats that were similar in shape to the conical basket hats. Some men added antlers or horns to their fur hats, others decorated their hats

Hats, which were worn by both men and women in the Plateau Culture Area, were made from such materials as reeds, fur, feathers, and shells. This Edward S. Curtis portrait shows a Wishram girl wearing a woven hat that resembles a basket. *(Library of Congress, Prints and Photographs Division [LC-USZ62-105382])*

People of the Plateau Culture Area acquired shells through trade with people of the coastal area. A Wishram girl is pictured wearing a beaded jacket, necklaces made from shells, and a bone nose-piercing in this 1910 photograph by Edward S. Curtis. *(Library of Congress, Prints and Photographs Division [LC-USZ62-64853])*

with feathers or shells. In the historical period, some groups like the Nez Perce adopted Plains-style feather bonnets.

Women wore either woven or buckskin skirts, aprons, and shirts. They also wore numerous decorations on their clothes as well as a variety of jewelry including earrings and necklaces. Shells traded from the coastal groups were an important decorative item. Dentalium shells were considered the most valuable. Both men and women wore their hair long, usually in two braids. Shells, feathers, and decorative strips of leather were sometimes woven into the braids. Both men and women in some of the Plateau groups practiced tattooing.

The Plateau people were very accomplished in beadwork. Traditionally, they worked with natural materials such as porcupine quills dyed in different colors, shells, animal teeth, and stones. With these items, they would make intricate patterns on their clothes, especially on clothes and

DENTALIA

Along the west coast of Vancouver Island and the Queen Charlotte Islands, a slender white univalve shellfish known as dentalium (plural dentalia) can be found in large numbers. Their shells were an important trading item for the Indians of the Northwest Coastal region. The shells, sometimes called money-tooth shells, were used in numerous ways by the people of the Plateau. They would string them together to form necklaces and would sew them onto all types of garments. The shells were traded by the Plateau tribes to Plains tribes and were found almost as far away as the Mississippi River.

moccasins worn on special occasions such as feast days and other important observances. Some of the men also wore special painted shirts on which the designs represented their dreams and visions. When glass beads became available through trade with non-Indians, Plateau beadwork designs became even more intricate and elaborate.

UTENSILS, TOOLS, AND WEAPONS

The Plateau people used a wide variety of materials to fashion the tools and utensils that they needed in everyday life. They used wood, stone, bone, antlers, other animal parts, bark, and a variety of plant fibers. An everyday implement such as a spoon might be carved from wood or from a horn of a buffalo or mountain goat. In its simplest form, half of a freshwater clamshell could be used as a spoon.

Revered among people of the Plateau, beadwork designs for clothing decoration often incorporated shells and animal teeth. Little Chief, an Umatilla, poses in front of a backdrop while wearing an elaborately beaded robe in this portrait ca. 1871–1907. *(National Archives and Records Administration)*

Many tools were made from a variety of stones. Arrowheads and spear points were made using flint, chert (a type of quartz), and obsidian. Plateau people would often trade for stone not available to them but needed for tools. More common stones such as basalt and granite were fashioned into hammers and pestles, which were used to grind roots, nuts, and meats. Stones were also used in sweat lodges and for cooking. Soups and stews were cooked by adding very hot stones from a fire to a waterproof basket or a bark bowl.

Stone knives were also important tools. A flint or obsidian bladed knife was extremely sharp. Some blades were shaped so they would fit in the hand without a handle. Other blades were attached to a wooden handle. Numerous scrapers were

BEAVER TOOTH KNIVES

Throughout the rivers and streams of the Plateau, beavers built their dams and lodges using the wood from trees they felled by gnawing through them with their extremely sharp and strong front teeth. The beaver was a valuable animal and it was trapped for its thick warm fur. When non-Indian fur traders reached the Plateau, they especially wanted as many beaver furs as the Indians could supply them. However, even before the arrival of non-Indian traders, beavers were highly sought after. Rather than waste those sharp front teeth, Plateau toolmakers inserted a beaver tooth into a wooden handle and created a very sharp and efficient knife.

needed for working hides and stripping roots and other fibers for making baskets. Many of these scrapers were made from bone or antlers.

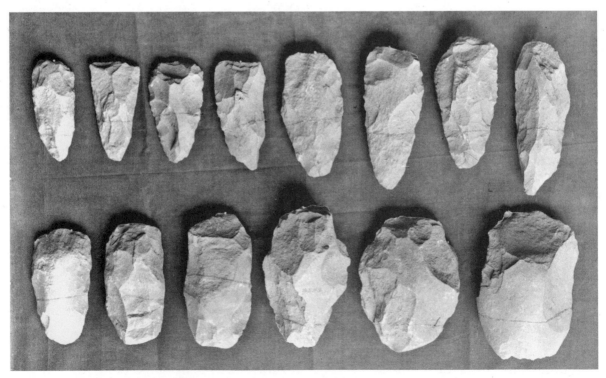

People of the Plateau created tools and weapons from such natural materials as wood, stone, animals, and plants. These Umatilla stone implements could have been used as arrowheads, spearpoints, pestles, or hammers. *(National Archives and Records Administration)*

Baskets served a number of important functions, including food storage, traps for fishing, clothing, and cooking implements. The five Okanagan baskets on the left of this image and the four Salish baskets on the right demonstrate the various geometric patterns woven into baskets by the people of the Plateau region. *(University of Washington)*

Probably the most widely used items on the Plateau were various types of baskets. The Plateau basket makers were some of the most accomplished among American Indians. They would fashion items from large baskets used to line storage pits to small baskets used to collect berries or other food. Baskets were also turned into fish traps, hats, moccasins, leggings, bags, waterproof bowls, and cooking pots. Many baskets had a woven pattern that might depict human or animal forms. Other baskets were woven with a variety of geometric patterns.

The patterns were made by using a variety of materials or by dyeing the materials using a number of plant substances such as berries and bark. The simplest baskets were made by weaving material in and out of a frame or by sewing pieces of birch bark together. More elaborate baskets were created by two methods—twining and coiling. A twined woven basket has numerous vertical pieces known as the warp. Once the warp is set, numerous pieces of material are wrapped around the warp; these pieces are called the weft. The weft ties the pieces of the warp together. In many Plateau baskets, both the warp and weft were of a soft material, giving the basket the feel and texture of coarse cloth.

Coiled baskets tended to be stiffer than twined baskets. A coiled basket was made by wrapping long strips of a material with a variety of natural and dyed grasses and other plant fibers. The underlying coil was usually made of a bundle of very fine red cedar tree roots, although other materials were used by some groups. As the coil was wrapped, it was attached to the coil below it. Many of the larger baskets used for gathering, storing, or transporting food were made using the coil method.

The universal weapon of the Plateau used for both hunting and warfare was the bow and arrow. There were three different types of bows that were common, and some groups used all three. The simplest bow was one that is called a longbow, which was made from a single tapered piece of wood. A shorter recurve bow that turned up at the ends was made of wood and had a number of layers of deer sinew glued to the outside of the curve. The sinew gave the bow strength and elasticity. The third type of bow was made using a rib bone of a buffalo or elk. The rib bows were very short and were used when the hunter was in heavy cover or had to shoot from the close quarters of a blind. All three bows used sinew strings.

Arrow shafts were made from a variety of woods such as alder or dogwood. The arrow maker used special grooved stones to straighten the arrows. Three feathers were attached to give the arrow stability in flight. Arrows had a variety of tips depending on their

Despite its simple design, which used only one piece of wood and sinew, the bow proved to be an effective weapon against both animals and humans. Paul Oyachen, a Spokane, poses while holding a bow and arrow for this portrait by Thomas W. Tolman. *(University of Washington)*

intended use. An arrow that was going to be used to hunt small game like rabbits and birds would not have any additional tip added to it. Other arrows would have several stone points varying in size depending on the targeted animal. The points were often secured using hemp string.

Hemp was a very important plant for the people of the Plateau. Its long fibers could be twisted into a strong string with many uses. Multiple strands of string could be twisted together to make rope, while a finer cord was used to make fishing nets. One hemp net has been found that is over six feet high and more than 300 feet long. Rocks were tied into the bottom of the net to keep it anchored down when it was stretched across a river.

Smaller nets were attached to poles and were just one of the many ways fish were caught in the Plateau region. A variety of specialized spears, fishing lines, traps, and weirs were also used. A fish weir is a manmade barrier built in a stream or river usually using rocks and sometimes wooden fences covered with mats.

Some of the most common fishing methods for people of the Plateau involved the use of nets, spears, and weirs. A Wishram man stands precariously on a cliff and leans over the water while attempting to net fish swimming in the river below in this 1910 Edwin S. Curtis photograph. *(Library of Congress, Prints and Photographs Division [LC-USZ62-46996])*

The weir forces migrating fish to swim through a narrow opening where they can be more easily trapped or speared. Many of the natural falls on the rivers were good places to catch the salmon and steelhead that filled the rivers each year.

TRANSPORTATION

Many people of the Plateau traveled great distances on foot. In winter, they would use snowshoes to get around. They also built a variety of boats—the two most common types were the bark canoe and the dugout. The dugout was made by taking a large

Dugout canoes were hollowed out by scraping the interior with stone tools and by setting a fire within the trunk being used to make the canoe. A Nez Perce man grips a pole and maneuvers a dugout canoe in this 1910 portrait by Edward S. Curtis. *(Library of Congress, Prints and Photographs Division [LC-USZ62-47015])*

log—pine logs were usually preferred—and shaping it into a long narrow boat. Once the outside of the boat had been shaped using a variety of stone and bone tools, the inside of the log had to be hollowed out. The same tools would be used to dig out the wood from the center of the log. Sometimes fire was used to speed up the process of removing wood from inside the boat. Rafts were also made out of logs.

Although the birch-bark canoe is often considered a creation of the Indians of the Northeast and Subarctic regions, it was also used by a number of groups in the Plateau area. Bark canoes were made by shaping large sheets of bark over a wooden frame. The seams between the sheets of bark were sewn together and then sealed with pitch to make the canoe watertight. Some Plateau people were known to make a canoe similar to a bark canoe but with animal skins instead of bark. These light canoes could be easily carried (portaged) around a waterfall or dangerous rapids. The dugout canoes were much heavier and tended to be used on large lakes and on the lower stretches of rivers where there were fewer obstacles to navigate.

In the late 1600s or early 1700s, horses arrived in the Plateau from Indian traders in the Great Basin. Within a relatively short time, many Plateau tribes adopted the horse and became successful horse breeders. Areas of the southern Plateau with vast expanses of lush grasslands for grazing were ideal for raising horses. The Cayuse, Nez Perce, Palouse, and some of the Yakama became some of the most accomplished horse breeders and riders. By the middle of the 19th century, white travelers in the Plateau region estimated that the Cayuse, Umatilla, and Walla Walla tribes had more than 20,000 horses. The Plateau tribes that kept and used horses quickly developed the skills to make all the needed tack for their horses. Saddles, bridles, and other items were often ornately decorated and covered with elaborate beadwork. Horses became a sign of wealth, and some individuals boasted herds of more than 1,000.

Brought to North America by the Spanish in the 1600s, horses were later introduced to the people of the Plateau by Indians of the Great Basin Culture Area. A Nez Perce man poses on horseback in this 1910 photograph by Edward S. Curtis. *(Library of Congress, Prints and Photographs Division [LC-USZ62-101259])*

4

Daily Life

The daily life of the Plateau Indians was tied into a seasonal round of activities that provided food and other materials needed to live. Often Plateau groups moved with the seasons to take advantage of the availability of food at different locations. Hunting, gathering, fishing, and winter survival might all take place in different geographical locations. Water was always an important consideration, and the people of the Plateau often followed rivers and streams as they moved about on their annual round of activities.

SPRING

Winter was often a hard time for the people of the Plateau. They had to depend on the food they had collected during the previous year to see them through the cold months. As those reserves were depleted, the coming of spring was an important signal that they had survived another year.

First Food Ceremonies

The close relation that the people of the Plateau felt with the spirit world around them was displayed in the many first food ceremonies they had during the year. As winter snows melted and the first green shoots of spring began to grow, people would harvest many of them that were edible. Plants such as cow parsnip, fireweed, barestem lomtium (also known as Indian celery), and others were gathered. Before the first greens of spring were eaten, a ceremony giving thanks to the spirits of the plants was held.

Ceremonies were often based around the seasons during which various animals were hunted. In this photograph from 1939, a woman cooks salmon outside a tipi in Kettle Falls, Washington, in a ceremony based on traditional Colville ceremonies. *(University of Washington)*

First food ceremonies were also held when the first salmon of spring was caught, when the first berries ripened in mid to late summer, and when the first nuts fell in the fall. They also held celebrations when the first deer was killed during a communal hunt, or at any other time when a food source was first used during that year. The ceremonies were intended to show respect for the spirits who were believed to provide the people with their food sources. A scarcity of plants to gather, the late arrival of the annual fish runs in the rivers, or a shortage of animals to hunt were all believed to be caused by the spirits because of some lack of ceremony or respect by the people.

Fishing

The most important event of the spring was when the first salmon reached the fishing location of a Plateau group. The further downstream the people lived, the earlier in the spring this would happen. Therefore, groups like the Cascades on the

Columbia and the Thompson on the Fraser were the first to see the salmon each spring. At the same time, it would take the fish quite a while to reach groups like the Kootenai or the Nez Perce who lived far upriver. Some upriver groups never got much in the way of salmon runs and had to depend on freshwater species and trade to provide the fish in their diets.

Salmon fishing often included the appointment of a salmon chief who would oversee the harvest of fish at a given site. At highly productive spots, such as Celilo Falls on the lower Columbia River people from different tribes would gather to fish. Once the First Salmon ceremony had been observed, the salmon chief would allow people to start fishing. A number of techniques were used to harvest salmon and other fish.

Various nets, traps, hooks, and spears were used. However, the most efficient way to catch migrating salmon was with a dip net, a bag-shaped net on the end of a long pole. Fishermen

Indians of the Plateau sometimes built a platform from which to fish. While this photograph is from 1941 (taken in Celio Falls, Oregon), the method has long been used. *(Library of Congress, Prints and Photographs Division [LC-USF33-013145-M2])*

A Wishram woman places salmon on a wooden plank in this photograph ca. 1910 taken by Edward S. Curtis—demonstrating the traditional ways salmon were dried in the sun. *(Library of Congress, Prints and Photographs Division [LC-USZ62-111293])*

would stand on rocks or build scaffolds that would allow them to stand over a narrow spot in a series of rapids. An experienced fisherman with a dip net could catch as many as 500 fish a day.

This may seem like a lot of fish, but it is estimated that people of the Plateau region, prior to the introduction of non-Native foods, ate between 400 and 450 pounds of fish per person a year. In addition to feeding all the members of his family, a fisherman who could produce a surplus of fish had a valuable good that could be traded with groups that were less fortunate in the quality of their fishing sites.

Once the fish were caught, there was much work to be done by the rest of the fisherman's family. The fish had to be cleaned as soon as possible. The heads were removed and often cooked to be eaten immediately. The eggs of the female fish called roe were set aside to be dried or smoked. The body of the salmon was skinned and spread open to dry in the sun or over fires. Some of the catch was completely dehydrated and pounded into a powder known as salmon flour.

SALMON FLOUR

Preserving enough salmon to get a family through the long winter and also having some for trade was a huge task. One ingenious method of preserving salmon meat was devised by the Plateau people. Fish were completely dehydrated (all moisture and oil removed) and then pounded into a fine powder called salmon flour. The flour was then pressed into large baskets lined with dried fish skins. The baskets weighed 90 to 100 pounds when full. The salmon flour would be added to soups and stews during the winter as well as traded. In the drying process, more than 60 percent of the weight of the fish is lost. Therefore, a 100-pound basket of salmon flour would represent as much as 250 pounds of fresh fish flesh. Some groups were known to add crushed berries to salmon flour to use it as a food source when they traveled to hunt or for other reasons.

Salmon was customarily pounded into a fine powder that was used as flour. A Wishram woman, holding a mortar and pestle, poses for this ca. 1910 portrait by Edward S. Curtis. (Library of Congress, Prints and Photographs Division [LC-USZ62-113089])

Chinook is one of the five varieties of salmon in addition to chum, coho, pink, and sockeye. This photograph shows a chinook salmon from the Columbia River in Washington State. *(University of Washington Libraries, Special Collections, UW 13234)*

Once the salmon camp was in full operation, a salmon feast was held by many Plateau groups. This would be a celebration of thanksgiving for the bountiful harvest that was in progress. It was a time when there was an abundance of food, and all could eat their fill and enjoy themselves, while at the same time giving thanks for their good fortune. For some groups, the salmon runs continued throughout the summer and even into the fall as the various species of salmon and steelhead trout entered the rivers at different times. There were five species of sea-run salmon plus the steelhead trout (a rainbow trout that spends most of its life in the ocean but spawns in freshwater) in the rivers of the Plateau. The five species of salmon are the chinook, chum, coho, pink, and sockeye. The chinook and sockeye were the most desirable. A chinook salmon weighs between 25 and 80 pounds. The sockeye are much smaller and average around seven pounds.

SUMMER

Fishing continued well into or through the summer for some groups. As the end of the annual fish runs approached, people

CAMAS ROOT

Camas, which comes from the Chinook word for "sweet" or "pleasant to the taste," is the bulb of a wild lily similar to the domesticated hyacinth plant. Camas grow in numerous locations in the Plateau region; where it was especially prolific, people from more than one tribe would come together to harvest it. Although the Plateau people did not plant camas, they did tend the areas where it grew naturally. They would harvest it in such a way as to encourage more plants in the future. They would also use fire to keep down undesirable plants that might overrun the camas.

The bulbs of the camas contain a complex sugar known as inulin that is hard to digest. By baking the bulbs before eating them, the inulin is broken down into the simple sugar fructose, which makes the roots very sweet. Camas and other similar roots were baked in large, rock-lined pit ovens. After the oven pit was created, a fire was built in it and kept going until the rocks were hot. Then the fire was allowed to die down. Layers of leaves and grass were then laid on the rocks. The camas bulbs or other roots would then be spread out in the oven. Old mats were then used to cover the roots. Next the oven was buried with a layer of dirt.

After the bulbs were cooked and dried, they could be ground into flour. Camas bulbs and flour were valuable on the Plateau. The flour, like other ground foods, could later be added to stews and soups. Camas flour was also combined with dried deer or elk meat and berries. All the ingredients were then mixed with animal fat or fish oil to make a highly nutritious and portable food called pemmican.

Indians of the Plateau region would often eat camas, the bulb of a wild lily, which could be baked and ground into fine flour and mixed with other foods to make a nutritious food called pemmican. A Yakama woman bends over to dig for roots in this 1909 photograph by Edward S. Curtis. *(Library of Congress, Prints and Photographs Division [LC-USZ62-99793])*

Chief Joseph, in an 1878 painting
by Cyrenius Hall

Rabbit's Skin Leggings, a member of
the Nez Perce tribe, in an 1832 painting
by George Catlin

Portrait of Fort Walla Walla

A tipi at Nez Perce Historical Park

Palouse Falls in eastern Washington State

Modoc basket

Klamath four stick game

C-3

Klikitat coiled basket

Nez Perce buffalo hide robe with Sacred Circle design

Nez Perce girl wearing a poncho

Statue in Lewiston, Idaho, of a mother bending down to show her daughter how to harvest camas

Chief of the Uma Pi Ma Tribe, a band of Umatilla

Levi Hold in front of the Nez Perce Reservation's Wolf Education and Research Center (WERC)

Leader of the Nez Perce Tribe holding a U.S. flag at a celebration
of the return of the Nez Perce to Oregon on June 12, 1997

The Black Lodge Singers have been nominated for multiple Grammy Awards

Rex Buck (left) and Thomas Morning Owl (right) performing a blessing ceremony for Sacajawea State Park near Pasco, Washington, on October 27, 2006

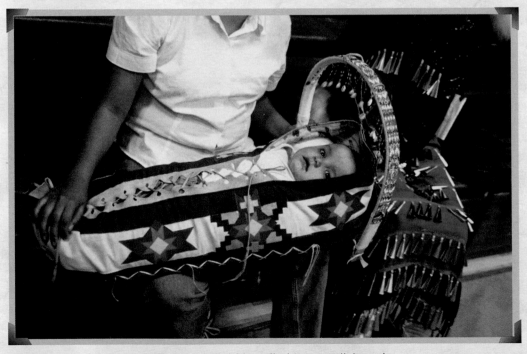

A Nez Perce child bundled in a cradleboard

had time for other activities. The vast quantities of fish had to be transported to the winter village and stored. Summer also saw the beginning of the annual trips to gather food. However, there was time for the appropriate seasonal festivals, games, and traveling to gatherings for trade.

Food Storage

Storing hundreds of pounds of fish and other food for a family was a large task that consumed much of the summer's labors. Dried salmon, salmon flour, and salmon roe were frequently put in storage pits. A pit would be dug near the winter dwelling and then lined with mats or special large baskets. The food would be carefully placed in the lined pits and then covered. Another mat or some other form of top would be placed over the food and then the entire pit would be covered with dirt to protect it from animals.

Other plant foods such as roots, nuts, and berries were dried either in the sun or in special ovens and then ground into powder. The various flourlike substances could be stored in large baskets in the winter houses or buried in storage pits. In addition to storage pits, some Plateau groups also built raised platforms for storage of dried foods.

Food Gathering

Scientists have identified as many as 135 different plants that were used by Plateau people for food, beverages, or seasoning. Roughly 30 of these plants are considered root vegetables. These included wild onions, carrots, and many other roots. Some roots were dried while others were baked, which transformed their chemical makeup. A few roots were especially important in the diet of the Plateau region—bitterroot, camas, and biscuit roots. They were important trade goods for groups that could gather a surplus of them.

Gathering berries was also an important summer activity. One of the most common berries in the area is the serviceberry, also called the Saskatoon berry in the Canadian part of the Plateau. The serviceberry comes from a plant known as the shadbush, which blooms with white flowers and is often one of the first bushes to bloom in spring. Many berries were eaten fresh after a first food ceremony. The surplus was usually dried. Serviceberries were sometimes dried individually and were similar to raisins. The berries were also formed into cakes and then dried.

Other fruits and berries were also picked. These included rose hips, high bush cranberries, chokecherries, huckleberries, wild strawberries, and raspberries. Some of the berries were naturally bitter and would be mixed with sweeter berries to make them more palatable. Like the serviceberries, those berries that were not eaten fresh were usually dried and stored for later.

Trade

Summer was also the time for trade. Throughout the Plateau region, people from different tribes would meet to trade whatever surplus or luxury goods they might have. Many of these gatherings were held in the same location every year. The French fur traders and later the trappers who moved into the western United States referred to these gatherings as rendezvous. It was also a time of relaxation when competitions of various kinds were held between members of different tribes.

One of the largest trade gatherings attended by Plateau people was held by the Shoshone in southwest Wyoming. Here, Indians from a variety of tribes and regions gathered together. It is likely that horses first found their way to the Plateau at one of these gatherings. Once the Plateau tribes had acquired horses, their trade routes expanded south to California and further east to the Great Plains. The success of the Nez Perce and Palouse in raising horses made Plateau horses an important trade commodity during the 18th century.

Games

A variety of games and competitions were held during the trade gatherings of the Plateau. Horse racing became an important event, and gambling on the races was popular. Before the horse, numerous other games of chance were popular. Woman played a dice game that involved four dice made from beaver teeth or the polished pieces made from the rib of a deer. One side of the dice was marked with stripes while the other had four circles. The players earned counters according to the number of dice that landed circle side up. Approximately 50 counters were used and a player had to acquire all the counters to win the game. The most popular gambling game of the Plateau is known as the stick game.

In addition to gambling games, a number of contests of skill and endurance were held. Wrestling matches, a variety of spear-tossing games, running races, and shooting matches were all held. In addition, the Plateau people played the game of shinny. Shinny was played with a hard wooden or leather ball and a stick with a curved end. Children, men, and coed teams of 10 to 20 people played shinny. However, in many groups,

THE STICK GAME

The stick game is played with two teams, usually from different groups, facing each other. An equal amount of goods and more recently money is put up by each team. The game is played with four round bone markers, two of which are wrapped with some sort of black string or thread, and 11 counting sticks. The counting sticks are used to keep score, while the bones are used to play the game. During the game, the two sides take turns concealing the bones in the hands of two of their team members. While the bone handlers place one of the marked and unmarked bones in their hands, both teams drum on logs arranged in front of them and sing special stick game songs.

The leader of the team known as a pointer then tries to guess how the bone handlers have concealed the bones in their hands. The pointer indicates a number of combinations by pointing with his or her thumb and fingers. If the pointer feels the bone handlers both have the marked bone in their left hands, he or she would point to the right with his or her index finger. By pointing in other directions and using the thumb as well, the pointer can indicate all the possible combinations of holding the bones. If the pointer guesses correctly, the bones come to his or her team. If the pointer guesses incorrectly, the bone-hiding team gets one stick for each incorrect guess. When one side wins all the counting sticks, the game is over and the winning team receives all the goods or money that has been wagered. The stick game is still popular among many Plateau tribes and is often played at powwows.

A group of women sit and play a stick game during the midsummer celebration in the Glacier National Park Reservation in Montana in this photograph from between 1910 and 1940. The stick game is still played by many Plateau tribes. *(Library of Congress, Prints and Photographs Division [LC-USZ62-106059])*

Mule deer, pictured here, were typically the most hunted animals in the Plateau region. *(U.S. Fish and Wildlife Service)*

shinny was played primarily by women. Two modern games have evolved from shinny: Field hockey and ice hockey both grew out of Europeans watching Indians play shinny. The word hockey comes from the French *hoquet,* which is the word for the crooked stick that shepherds carry.

FALL
Hunting
For most Plateau tribes, hunting was secondary to fishing as a food source. However, those groups that lived where fish were less abundant had to depend more on hunting. Even so, all Plateau groups held successful hunters in high regard. A wide variety of animals were hunted for both meat and hides. These ranged from small squirrels to large animals such as buffalo and elk. The most hunted animal was the mule deer.

Deer were hunted in different ways. Sometimes, a single hunter stalked a single deer and other times a whole village, or even larger group, participated in a deer drive where many animals would be killed. In the large deer drives, the hunters would hide by a brush corral or a natural enclosure and wait for the deer to be driven to them. Among some groups, dogs were included in the drive as well as used to track individual deer.

Before the coming of the horse, buffalo were only available to those on the eastern edge of the Plateau or by trading for their hides. After the horse became the primary means of transportation for the Plateau, many hunters traveled to the Plains to hunt buffalo. They would often live off the buffalo they killed and only bring home the valuable hides. It was at this time that many Plateau groups adopted the more portable Plains-style tipi to live in.

A Deer Hunt

All hunting was taken seriously by Plateau hunters. If a group of hunters agreed to cooperate in a deer hunt, there were a number of preparations that were necessary before they began. First, a hunt leader would be selected. This would be someone whose hunting skills were respected by all the members of the group. Next, the hunters would often spend time in their sweat lodges. The use of the sweat lodge had two purposes. It helped eliminate the hunter's human scent. The sweat lodge ritual also prepared the hunters mentally and spiritually for the hunt. Most American Indians believed that all aspects of their world were under the supervision of the spirit world. A successful hunt required the cooperation of the appropriate spirit to succeed.

The hunt would be organized according to the directions of the hunt leader, and a small group of hunters might work a specific area where some would serve as drivers while others would conceal themselves and wait for the deer to come within range of their bows and arrows. When a deer was killed, the hunting group would butcher the deer and eat the liver at the kill site. This was accompanied by proper prayers to the spirit of the deer for letting itself be taken. The hunter who shot the deer first would be in charge of dividing the animal among the group. It was important not to waste any part of the deer as that would anger the spirits.

Once the Plateau tribes began traveling to the Plains to hunt, conflict between the Plateau hunters and the Plains tribes increased. The Plains Indians saw the Plateau hunters as encroaching on their hunting grounds. Before the coming of the horse, there was very little conflict for the Plateau tribes or on the Plains.

Many animals were also hunted and trapped specifically for their fur. These included foxes, wolves, coyotes, mountain lions, and smaller animals such as beavers, weasels, and mink. Porcupines were hunted for their quills, which were used to decorate clothing and other objects. Rabbits and hares were also hunted for both meat and fur. In the southern Plateau region, large groups would often hunt hares by driving them toward a long net set up to trap them. Rabbit and hare skins were often cut into long strips and woven to make warm blankets and outer garments for protection from the cold of winter.

Gathering

The gathering of plants that began with the first ripe berries of summer continued into the fall. Late-ripening berries and fruits were harvested, as well as a variety of nuts. Hazelnuts and acorns were collected where they were available, but the most important nut crop on the Plateau was the pine nut from the white-bark pine. Whole groups of people would travel up to higher elevations in the fall to collect pine nuts. They were usually roasted in their shells and were a favorite snack food for the people of the Plateau.

WINTER
Survival

Winter in the Plateau region can bring very cold temperatures and snow. Life in the winter villages of the Plateau tribes was often spent inside around the fires making tools, clothing, and other objects. Winter was also the time for telling stories. The stories were told around the winter fires and were intended to instruct young people and remind older people about the spiritual and mythological history of their tribe and the lands in which they lived. The stories were also intended to instruct people about proper behavior, often including a lesson.

Storytelling was considered an important skill, and someone good at telling the tribe's stories was a respected member of the community. Often stories had set patterns that were repeated as the story was told. A really accomplished storyteller might take as many as three sessions on consecutive nights to tell one of his or her more complicated tales. Many of the stories included spirits, and one of the most frequently included in stories was the coyote. The spirit coyote was seen as having a special role in helping create the world of the Plateau people. In some stories, coyote helped the people. In others, he played upon people's weaknesses like pride and greed to teach them a lesson.

Winter Spirit Dance

There were numerous religious observances throughout the year for most Plateau tribes. One of the more important ones was the Winter Spirit Dance. This ceremony took place at various times during the winter depending on the tribe. Some tribes held the

COYOTE SAVES ALL THE PLANTS AND ANIMALS

Long ago, a huge sea monster swam up the Great River (Columbia) until he came to a series of rapids he could not pass. At this point, the monster opened its mouth and began sucking in huge quantities of food. First it ate all the salmon. Then it devoured all the other fish in the river. But this still did not fill its great stomach. The sea monster then began to inhale all the nearby land animals and edible plants. The people who saw this became very concerned as it became harder for them to find anything to eat.

Some of the people called on the coyote spirit to help them. Coyote had helped create the people and did not want to see them starve so he decided to kill the sea monster. First, Coyote gathered some kindling for making a fire and flint to create the spark to start the fire. He then got a long length of vine. He tied one end of the vine to the rocks near where the sea monster was. The other end he tied around his waist. Coyote then made his presence known to the monster by shouting insults at it and calling it names.

The monster was angered by Coyote and sucked him into its great belly with all the plants, animals, and fish that it had already eaten. Coyote then took out his kindling and flints and started a fire in the monster's belly. The heat and smoke of the fire bothered the monster and it opened its mouth and tried to blow out the fire. When the monster's mouth opened, Coyote began throwing out everything the monster had swallowed. As the fire grew, the fat that lined the monster's stomach began to drip into the fire and the fire grew. As Coyote threw out the last of the plants and creatures in the monster's stomach, the monster began to die. Coyote knew he had little time to escape and quickly pulled himself out using the vine that he had tied around his waist. When the monster finally died, it was washed back down the river to the sea. The people were happy that Coyote had saved them.

(This story was adapted by the authors from a variety of sources.)

ceremony to coincide with the winter solstice in December. Others held it later in January or February. For some, the dancing lasted a fixed period of time from three to eight nights in length. Other groups started in midwinter and continued until half the snow on the nearby mountains had disappeared, which signaled that spring would soon arrive.

The Winter Spirit Dance had a number of functions. It was in part the celebration of the beginning of the new year and a time of thanksgiving. It was also when individuals renewed their personal contacts with the spirit world. All those who had gained a spirit contact from a vision quest or in some other way had their own spirit song. During the ceremony, which was usually started by one of the shamans in the group, each person would dance and sing his or her spirit song.

Winter Hunting

Although fall was the most important hunting season, many hunters tried to supply fresh meat to their families and villages during the winter. Elk and deer that lived in the mountains were forced by deep snow to move down into the valleys in the

During winter, elk would travel from the mountains to lower elevations in order to find food. In this photograph, elk graze against a backdrop of mountains. *(U.S. Fish and Wildlife Service)*

winter. This often made it easier for the hunters of the Plateau to succeed in providing food in the winter. This was especially important if a group was running low on the food they had preserved to get through the winter.

In addition to hunting for food, a number of small animals were hunted and trapped during the winter for their fur. Beavers, mink, ermine, bobcats, foxes, among others, all had their thickest fur during the winter months. These furs were used for warm clothing, bedding, and as decoration on some ceremonial outfits. A simple snare (a loop of cord) set along a known animal run was the most common type of trap. After the coming of Europeans traders to the region, furs became important trade items.

5

The Coming of Europeans

FIRST CONTACTS

The first Europeans to visit the Plateau region may have been fur traders and priests toward the end of the 18th century. Major exploration of the region did not begin until the area became part of the United States and President Thomas Jefferson sent the Lewis and Clark expedition to explore the area in 1805. Despite the lack of Europeans in the Plateau region, the Indians felt the impact of European goods, animals, and diseases as early as the 17th century.

DISEASE

Plateau Indians had been isolated from the diseases of Asia and Europe for more than 10,000 years before the first Europeans from Spanish California and Russian Alaska began visiting the Northwest Coast. Due to this lack of exposure, these Indians had no resistance to diseases spread by these first visitors. Measles, mumps, and especially smallpox proved deadly to the Plateau tribes even without their ever having been in contact with a European. Disease spread up the rivers from the coastal Indians and killed a huge portion of the people of the Plateau. Some have estimated that between the first epidemic and the arrival of Lewis and Clark, the population of the Plateau may have been cut in half.

Some groups ceased to exist at this time, and the survivors joined neighboring groups. Other tribes reduced their range and the number of their villages as survivors joined together. The tribes farthest from the coast and in the northernmost part of the region were spared the earliest epidemics. In 1780, a devastating epidemic raged through the Plains tribes and then traveled up the Missouri River until it crossed the Rocky Mountains and affected the people on the eastern edge of the Plateau. Some attribute the increased mobility brought by the introduction of the horse with the rapid spread of the 1780 epidemic and others. Smallpox epidemics continued across the Plateau into the 19th century.

HORSES

By the later years of the 17th century, the Spanish had moved north out of Mexico and established settlements along the Rio Grande in New Mexico as well as in what is now Arizona and California. The major activity of these Spanish settlements was livestock raising. Sheep, cattle, and horses were all brought into the Southwest. During the 17th century, the Pueblo Indians of the Rio Grande Valley were forced to help the Spanish settlers on their ranches. Other Indians of the Southwest including the Apache, Navajo, and Ute were known to raid Spanish settlements and were probably the first Indians in the West to have horses. The first horses to reach the Plateau most likely came north via already established trade routes.

Horses were introduced to the people of the Plateau by the Spanish during the 17th century. This ca. 1897 drawing by Frederic Remington depicts Francisco Vásquez de Coronado and Spanish soldiers traveling with horses. *(Library of Congress, Prints and Photographs Division [LC-USZ62-37993])*

In the late 1600s, Plateau Indians acquired horses that were abandoned by Spanish settlers. The popularity of horses in the region endured, as evidenced by this photograph from 1898, in which a group of Salish men herd horses in Montana. *(University of Washington)*

At first, horses were a novelty for the people of the Plateau as they knew nothing of riding or breeding them. Other than a few dogs, domestic animals did not exist in the Plateau region. However, in 1680, Pueblo Indians revolted against Spanish settlers, forcing many to retreat to Mexico for a period of time. During the Pueblo Revolt, many horses were left behind and gathered up by the Indians. With this increased availability of horses, the people of the Plateau, especially the Nez Perce, Cayuse, and Palouse, acquired more horses and soon became accomplished riders and breeders.

FUR TRADE

Among the important resources that North America provided for Europe from the 1600s onward were fur and leather. The Dutch, French, and English became involved in the fur trade in eastern North America. In western North America, the Russians established trading posts in Alaska. By the end of the 18th century,

Spain, Russia, England, and the United States were all competing to establish trade along the northwestern coast. Although none of these traders traveled inland, their goods did. When the Lewis and Clark expedition crossed the Plateau region in the early years

THE APPALOOSA

Palouse and Nez Perce became known across the Plateau and out into the Plains for their expertise as horsemen and breeders. No one is sure exactly which tribe first started selecting for spotted horses. These spotted horses became known as Appaloosas. The name may have originated with the Palouse or it may have come from the fact that some of the Nez Perce lived along the Palouse River. In either case, these horses became the trademark of the Nez Perce and since 1938 have been recognized as a specific breed. In the 19th century, when the Nez Perce were defeated by the U.S. Army and forced to move onto small reservations, many of their horses were confiscated by the army. In the last part of the 20th century, interest among the Nez Perce in the Appaloosa horse was renewed, and many modern members of the tribe proudly raise the horses made famous by their ancestors.

Notable for their spots, Appaloosa horses were a special breed created by the Nez Perce and Palouse tribes of the Plateau region. Two Nez Perce men pose atop Appaloosa horses for an 1879 photograph taken in southeastern Idaho. *(National Archives and Record Administration)*

of the 19th century, they found the Indians there already had numerous European and American manufactured goods.

An Umatilla chief poses against a painted backdrop of tipis in this photograph ca. 1871–1907. He wears a Hudson Bay Company blanket, which was a highly traded commodity during the time. *(National Archives and Record Administration)*

Trade had long been established between the coastal and Plateau tribes. Once manufactured trade goods arrived on the coast, it was a natural progression for those goods to be traded up the Columbia and other rivers of the region. Lewis and Clark found many Plateau Indians already had iron knives and hatchets, blankets, cloth to replace their deerskin clothing, and other goods. Once Lewis and Clark explored routes into the Plateau region, fur traders soon followed. The fur traders along the coast and those who came to the region later were often followed or accompanied by missionaries who wanted to convert the Indians to Christianity. There is evidence that some Christian ideas reached the Plateau along with the trade goods from the coast. However, direct missionary activity in the region did not take place until after Lewis and Clark had explored the territory.

6

The Plateau in the Nineteenth Century

LEWIS AND CLARK

In 1803, the United States negotiated the Louisiana Purchase whereby the United States acquired all the land claimed by France between the Mississippi River and the Rocky Mountains. During this period, President Thomas Jefferson and others were interested in expanding the United States beyond the Rocky Mountains to the Pacific Ocean. To learn more about the Northwest and to establish a claim to the area, President Jefferson sent Captain Meriwether Lewis and Lieutenant William Clark to explore the region in 1804. The Lewis and Clark expedition, known as the Corps of Discovery, left St. Louis, Missouri, in May 1804. They traveled up the Missouri River and built Fort Mandan, in present-day North Dakota, where they spent the winter. In the spring, they hired a French-Canadian trapper named Toussaint Charbonneau to serve as an interpreter. It is said that Toussaint had recently won an Indian woman named Sacajawea in a bet. Sacajawea became Charbonneau's wife and servant and joined the expedition with her husband.

Lieutenant William Clark was sent with Captain Meriwether Lewis by President Thomas Jefferson to explore the region of the United States acquired through the Louisiana Purchase of 1803. *(Library of Congress, Prints and Photographs Division [LC-USZ62-10609])*

A ca. 1903 portrait by C. W. Peale of Meriwether Lewis, who was sent with Lieutenant William Clark by President Thomas Jefferson to explore the region of the United States acquired through the Louisiana Purchase in 1803. *(Library of Congress, Prints and Photographs Division [LC-USZ62-20214])*

Lewis and Clark returned to Saint Louis in September 1806 after meeting many of the tribes of the southern Plateau. Their reports established a claim to the area for the United States. The reports the two explorers gave also excited many land-hungry people in the United States.

FUR TRADERS

Even before Lewis and Clark explored the southern Plateau, Alexander MacKenzie had traveled through Canada to the Pacific in 1793. MacKenzie was a member of the North West

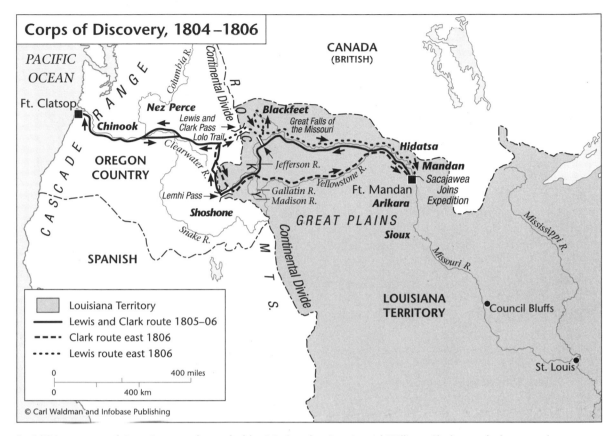

Corps of Discovery, 1804–1806

PACIFIC OCEAN

Ft. Clatsop

CANADA (BRITISH)

Columbia R.

Continental Divide

CASCADE RANGE

Chinook

Nez Perce

Lewis and Clark Pass

Lolo Trail

Clearwater R.

Blackfeet

Great Falls of the Missouri

R O C K Y

OREGON COUNTRY

Lemhi Pass

Jefferson R.

Hidatsa

Mandan

Sacajawea Joins Expedition

Gallatin R.

Madison R.

Yellowstone R.

Ft. Mandan

Arikara

Shoshone

Snake R.

GREAT PLAINS

Sioux

Continental Divide

M T S.

SPANISH

LOUISIANA TERRITORY

Missouri R.

Mississippi R.

Council Bluffs

St. Louis

Louisiana Territory
Lewis and Clark route 1805–06
Clark route east 1806
Lewis route east 1806

0   400 miles
0   400 km

© Carl Waldman and Infobase Publishing

In 1804 a group of American explorers led by Meriwether Lewis and William Clark traveled across the Plateau to the Pacific Ocean and back, establishing a U.S. claim to the region.

Company, which was competing in Canada for furs with the Hudson Bay Company. In 1807, the North West Company established its first trading post among the Kootenai of the northern Plateau region, which Canadians referred to as New Caledonia. In 1811, the North West Company opened a trading post at Fort Astoria near the mouth of the Columbia River. The following year, MacKenzie opened another trading post among the Nez Perce.

Many Plateau tribes were quick to devote effort to meeting the demand for furs. However, the Nez Perce were not interested in trapping. Instead, they found that it was much more efficient to trade their surplus horses. They either directly swapped horses with the fur traders for manufactured goods

SACAJAWEA (SACAGEWEA)
(1784 [or 1787] to 1812 [or 1884])

Sacajewea was a member of the Shoshone tribe who was probably born in 1784 (although some report her birth year as 1787). When she was about 12 years old, she was kidnapped during a raid by Hidatsa warriors. In 1804, according to most reports, the French-Canadian trader Toussaint Charbonneau won her in a gambling game, although others have argued he may have instead purchased her. When Charbonneau signed on to serve as a guide and interpreter for the Corps of Discovery, he persuaded Lewis and Clark to allow Sacajawea to join the group.

When the expedition left Fort Mandan in April 1805, Sacajawea traveled with her two-month-old son Jean Baptiste Charbonneau (known as Pomp) on his cradleboard. Much has been written about Sacajawea's role in the expedition, some of it created by the overactive imaginations of writers who wished to romanticize Indians in general and Sacajawea specifically. Putting the fancies of writers aside, the facts recorded in the journals kept by those on the expedition, especially those of William Clark, depict her as key to the expedition.

When the explorers were short of food, Sacajawea showed them how to gather and

A statue in City Park in Portland, Oregon, by Alice Cooper portrays Sacajawea, a member of the Shoshone tribe, who accompanied French-Canadian trader Touissant Charbonneau and served as interpreter and guide for the Lewis and Clark expedition. Sacajawea traveled with the expedition from 1804 to 1806 and provided indispensable insights into Native culture for Lewis and Clark. *(Library of Congress, Prints and Photographs Division [LC-USZ62-93141])*

or indirectly traded for furs with tribes that wanted horses and then traded the furs for goods. By the 1840s, fur-bearing animals of the Plateau had become extremely difficult to find, and the end of the fur trade was in sight. As the fur trade came to an end, settlers began to look toward the Northwest and presented a serious threat to the Indians of the Plateau.

prepare local plants and roots. In addition, Sacajawea was invaluable in helping the expedition peacefully come into contact with many Indian tribes. This was most important when the exploratory group reached the headwaters of the Missouri River and needed to travel overland across the Rocky Mountains. As the group tried to negotiate with Cameahwait, a Shoshone chief, Sacajawea recognized the chief as her brother. Because of their relationship, Cameahwait provided horses and guides to the expedition to get them over the mountains and to the headwaters of the Columbia River, where they could build boats and travel downstream to the Pacific Ocean.

Once they reached the Plateau, Sacajawea was able to communicate with the Nez Perce and other tribes they came in contact with through sign language. In the winter of 1805–06, the expedition built a small outpost known as Fort Clatsop on the banks of the lower Columbia River near present-day Astoria, Oregon. When a small group set out to scout the river, Sacajawea was allowed to accompany them as she did not want to travel this far without seeing the ocean.

After spending the winter at Fort Clatsop, Lewis and Clark split their group and returned east via two different routes. Lewis stayed south and descended the Yellowstone River. Clark took a more northern route and descended the Marias River to the Missouri. Sacajawea and Charbonneau traveled with Clark. When the two groups reunited, Sacajawea and Charbonneau left the expedition. Lewis and Clark returned to Saint Louis in September 1806 to a heroes' welcome.

What happened to Sacajawea after that is subject to controversy. It is known that she and Charbonneau went to Saint Louis in 1807, where they tried farming. They soon left for the Plains, leaving Pomp with William Clark, who agreed to care for him and see that he was educated. One version of the story has Sacajawea dying of disease in 1812 while at Fort Manuel, a fur-trading post in present-day South Dakota. Another version states she traveled around the prairies until she settled on the Wind River Reservation where she lived until she was 100 years old. Most scholars give more credibility to the first story. Whichever story is true, all agree that Sacajawea made an important contribution to the opening of the Northwest to white settlers and is still one of the best-known American Indian women.

OREGON TRAIL

In early 1842, a group of settlers led by Doctor Elijah White reached what would be called Oregon City, Oregon. The route they followed became known as the Oregon Trail. By 1850, more than 11,000 settlers had traveled the trail and settled in what was originally called the Oregon Territory and later became the states of Idaho, Washington, and Oregon. The wagon routes along the Oregon Trail were easy targets for roving bands of warriors from a number of Plateau tribes.

In 1846, the United States and Great Britain reached an agreement on conflicting claims on the Plateau. The two countries agreed on a boundary that followed the line set by 49 degrees north latitude. This gave the southern part of the Plateau official status as a territory of the United States. Soon the federal government became involved in Indian relations on the Plateau below the 49th parallel. As more and more settlers rushed in, they soon outnumbered the Indians and were making demands for land claimed by the various tribes.

From the 1840s to the 1870s, many travelers to the northwestern United States followed a route called the Oregon Trail. This ca. 1930 drawing by William Henry Jackson depicts life on the Oregon Trail, which was marked by travelers in stagecoaches and covered wagons. *(Library of Congress, Prints and Photographs Division [LC-USZ62-94187])*

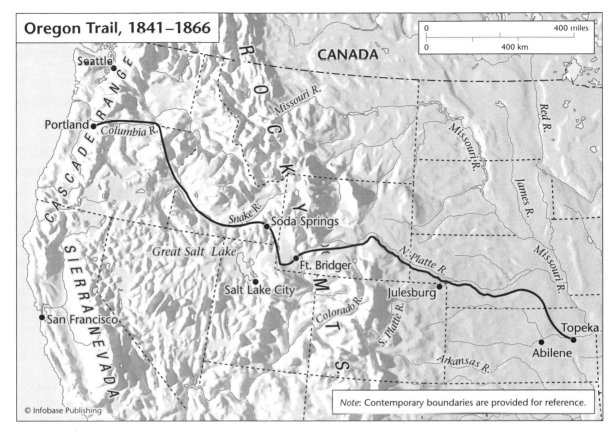

Once the United States took possession of the Northwest in 1846, non-Indian settlers began to stream into the region using the Oregon Trail.

WALLA WALLA TREATIES

In 1853, the U.S. Congress created Washington Territory, and Isaac I. Stevens was appointed governor. Part of his responsibility was to handle the Indians living in the territory. In 1855, Governor Stevens called together many tribal leaders in hopes of establishing a series of reservations in the territory. He hoped to lessen conflicts between the white settlers and the Indians.

The negotiations were often long as tribal leaders found it difficult to give up large tracts of land that had been their territory far into the distant past. However, Governor Stevens and others eventually wore them down and got them to agree to settle their people on a number of reservations. The Cayuse,

Umatilla, and Walla Walla agreed to share a reservation along the Umatilla River. The Palouse and Yakama were to settle on a reservation on the Yakima River. The Nez Perce were still the largest tribe on the Plateau and received their own reservation in the area of the Clearwater, Salmon, and Snake Rivers. Later, both the Spokan and Coeur d'Alene would also be forced to accept reservations.

It took four years before the U.S. Congress ratified the Walla Walla treaties, as these resettlement agreements were called, and almost immediately trouble began. The treaties called for payments in goods and money to the tribes, but such payments could not begin without Congress's approval. At the same time, white settlers and land speculators immediately started moving in on land that had been given up by the treaties. The discovery of gold in 1860 in the Canadian part of the Plateau caused even more problems as prospectors rushed from the depleted goldfields in California to the Plateau. The miners disregarded Indian property rights, and a number of small conflicts arose.

WAR ON THE PLATEAU

From the time the United States took over the Plateau region in 1846 until the defeat of the Nez Perce in 1877, a number of small wars between Plateau tribes and the U.S. Army were fought. The various wars continued the official program of reducing the amount of land held by the tribes. The Cayuse, Yakama, Coeur d'Alene, Modoc, Palouse, Walla Walla, Umatilla, Columbia, and other tribes at various times all fought with and were defeated by the U.S. Army. During these conflicts, the Nez Perce remained neutral or even helped the U.S. government by supplying horses and scouts when they fought the traditional enemies of the Nez Perce.

However, over the years, the relationship between the Nez Perce and the U.S. government became strained as settlers, miners, and government officials all tried to take pieces of the Nez Perce reservation. In 1873, President Ulysses S. Grant promised the Nez Perce that they could hold onto their lands in the Wallowa Valley of western Oregon. Only two years later, Grant gave into political pressure from white settlers and government officials in Oregon and reversed his position on Wallowa Valley. In May 1877, General Oliver O. Howard called together all the leaders of the Nez Perce and told them that all

This 1878 wooden engraving from *Frank Leslie's Illustrated Newspaper* portrays Indians receiving annual supplies. *(Library of Congress, Prints and Photographs Division [LC-USZC2-768])*

bands of the tribe must move onto a much-reduced reservation within 30 days.

Chief Joseph of the Wallowa band gathered his people together and rounded up their cattle and horses. Despite the fact that the rivers they would have to cross were swollen from the spring runoff, they tried to comply with the army's demands. Many of the calves and young horses drowned crossing the rivers. Once across the rivers, a number of Nez Perce bands came together on the Camas Prairie near Lake Tolo. As the people and the livestock took a much-needed rest before moving onto the reservation, some of the young men among them decided to seek revenge against a group of white men who had killed their relatives.

The young warriors killed four white men who were known to have killed Indians without provocation. This small raid set off what has become known as the Nez Perce War. Chief Joseph argued for a peaceful solution, but many of his fellow chiefs and warriors did not want to give in and move onto the reservation. The Nez Perce War consisted of a small force of Nez Perce warriors along with their families defeating and avoiding much larger army forces. The Indians fled from Oregon

General O. O. Howard is depicted in this 1877 portrait from *Harper's Weekly*. General Howard ordered all the members of the Nez Perce tribe to relocate to the Nez Perce reservation in May 1877. *(Library of Congress, Prints and Photographs Division [LC-USZ62-130186])*

Chief Joseph of the Wallowa band of the Nez Perce is depicted in this 1903 portrait. Chief Joseph led his people away from the Nez Perce Reservation beginning in 1877, in what is known as the Flight of the Nez Perce. *(Library of Congress, Prints and Photographs Division [LC-USZ61-2088])*

through Idaho, Wyoming, and Montana for 1,700 miles for more than four months.

The fighting started on June 17, 1877, when 100 soldiers came upon a Nez Perce group at White Bird Canyon in Idaho. In the Indian camp, there were approximately 50 warriors and numerous women and children. When the Nez Perce sent out an envoy under a white flag to talk to the soldiers, one eager soldier shot him. The Nez Perce fired back and killed two soldiers. In the battle that followed, the outnumbered Nez Perce routed the soldiers. They killed 34 and wounded four while only two of their own warriors were wounded. The Nez Perce were able to capture some of the army's horses, as well as collecting 63 guns and a good supply of ammunition that would prove very valuable in the long struggle that followed.

After the battle, the Nez Perce moved on and were soon joined by many other members of their tribe. At its largest, there were more than 700 Nez Perce moving at will through the mountains of the West. Of that number, there were only about 150 able-bodied warriors, the rest consisting of women, children, and old men.

On July 11 and 12, 1877, the next battle was fought between the Nez Perce and the army. At the Battle of Clearwater River, General Howard surprised the Nez Perce camp and seemed to have the upper hand with his force of 400 soldiers. Once again, the Nez Perce showed their superiority as fighters. The Indian warriors were able to hold off the army while their families escaped. The Nez Perce then retreated, leaving 13 dead and almost 40 wounded soldiers behind. The Nez Perce lost four fighters and had six wounded. It would be almost a month before the army would catch up with the Nez Perce again as they had decided to head east in hopes of allying themselves with their friends the Crow.

As the army sent even more troops into the field, the tide began to turn. At Big Hole Valley in Montana, on August 9, 1877, 89 Nez Perce, only 12 of them warriors, died in a surprise attack. Back in Idaho at Camas Meadows, 10 days later, some of the Nez Perce turned the tables on the army, conducting a raid on their main camp and running off with as many as 200 of their pack animals. This gave the main Nez Perce group enough time to pass through the recently created Yellowstone Park. They then turned north into Montana, where they hoped to find help among the Crow.

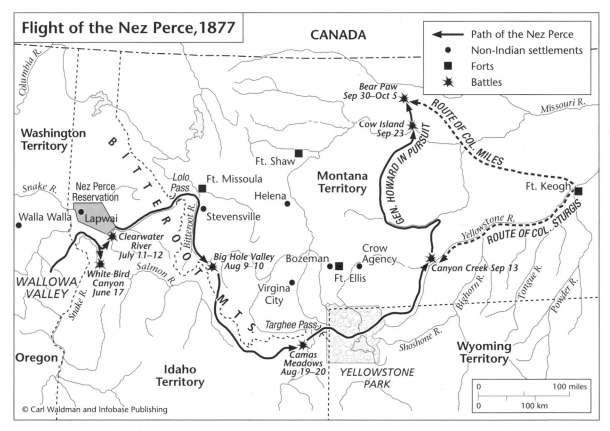

For almost four months in 1877, the Nez Perce led by Chief Joseph evaded the U.S. Army, as they attempted to escape forced relocation onto a reservation.

The Nez Perce War, which lasted from 1863 to 1877, pitted the Nez Perce against agents of the U.S. government in numerous battles through the Plateau region. In this 1877 painting, Nez Perce sit on the slope of a canyon and observe the ensuing battle. *(Library of Congress, Prints and Photographs Division [LC-USZ62-130186])*

General N. A. Miles is depicted in this 1877 portrait from *Harper's Weekly.* General Miles surrounded the Nez Perce led by Chief Joseph during the Nez Perce war on September 30, 1877. *(Library of Congress, Prints and Photographs Division [LC-USZ62-130186])*

When the Nez Perce learned that the Crow wanted no part of their war, the remaining chiefs decided to try and make a run for Canada. Many of the Sioux, who had helped defeat General George Armstrong Custer at the battle of the Little Big Horn in 1876, had earlier fled to Canada. On September 13, 1877, the increasingly smaller group of Nez Perce was again caught by the army at Canyon Creek where it joins the Yellowstone River. Again, the Indians gave the army the slip and made their last dash for the border. At Cow Island on the Missouri River 10 days later, those still traveling with Chief Joseph found a cache of supplies and stopped to take what they could and rest up for the final 50 miles to the Canadian border.

Chief Joseph had scouts keep a careful watch on their back trail and knew that pursuit from that direction was not close. What he did not realize was that the army was communicating by telegraph to position a force between the Nez Perce and the border. On September 30, Colonel Nelson A. Miles, with fresh troops, surprised the Nez Perce at the foot of the Bear Paw Mountains. Miles surrounded the group and waited for General Howard and the rest of the army. Each night, more Indian warriors snuck out of camp to avoid being captured. When Howard arrived on October 4, Chief Joseph was the only chief left in camp. He decided it was time to surrender.

On October 5, Chief Joseph rode out with a small contingent of warriors walking behind him. He surrendered to Miles and Howard. As he offered his surrender, there were only 350 women and children and about 80 warriors left in the Nez Perce camp. Many of the women and children had died at Bear Paw and at other battles along the way. Some of the surviving warriors had snuck off to Canada or disappeared among

In this 1877 wood engraving from *Frank Leslie's Illustrated Paper*, Chief Joseph of the Nez Perce hands his rifle to General N. A. Miles as an act of surrender. In a famous speech, Chief Joseph surrendered to the U.S. government on behalf of the Nez Perce on September 30, 1877. *(Library of Congress, Prints and Photographs Division [LC-USZC4-8391])*

Indian tribes of the Plains. The words spoken by Chief Joseph as he surrendered are some of the most famous spoken by an American Indian.

After their capture, the remaining Nez Perce were first sent to Kansas and then to Oklahoma. They were not allowed to return home to the Plateau for many years. Chief Joseph was never allowed to return to his homeland in the Wallowa Valley despite the fact that he lived until 1904 and visited both presidents William McKinley and Theodore Roosevelt in Washington, D.C.

"I Will Fight No More Forever"

"Tell General Howard I know his heart. I am tired of fighting. Our chiefs are killed. . . . The old men are all dead. It is the young men who say yes or no. He who led on the young men is dead. It is cold, and we have no blankets. The little children are freezing to death. My people, some of them, have run away to the hills and have no blankets, no food; no one knows where they are—perhaps freezing to death. I want time to look for my children and see how many I can find. Maybe I shall find them among the dead."

Chief Joseph then turned to his own people and continued, "Hear me, my chiefs. I am tired. My heart is sick and sad. From where the sun now stands, I will fight no more forever."

A group of Nez Perce men sit for an 1877 portrait before their forced relocation to Indian Territory (present-day Oklahoma). After the surrender of the Nez Perce, the remaining members of the tribe were forced to relocate to Indian Territory without first returning to their traditional home in the Plateau. *(University of Washington)*

LOSING MORE LAND

As the 19th century came to a close, the official policy of the U.S. government was to try and have the remaining Indians of the Plateau and throughout the country become members of the mainstream culture. This policy was officially known as assimilation. One of the ways the government attempted to do this was through the General Allotment Act of 1887, also known as the Dawes Act, after the senator (Henry L. Dawes) who was its primary sponsor. Under the Dawes Act, reservations around the country were to be divided up and allotted to individual members of each reservation's tribe. After the members of the tribe received their allotments, any excess land could be sold by the U.S. government.

Some tribal lands on the Plateau had already been allotted to individual Indians. The Nez Perce were the first Plateau tribe to be affected by the Dawes Act. What happened to them set the stage for the other reservations of the region. The Nez Perce were still more interested in raising cattle and horses than becoming farmers. This did not matter to the U.S. government, which went forward with its plan to divide up the reservation into numerous small farms.

The first task was for U.S. officials to identify who was actually a member of the Nez Perce tribe. After an extensive census was taken, it was determined that there were 2,278 individual members of the tribe. Every man, woman, and child received an allotment of 80 acres. This took up 182,240 acres of the reservation. The tribe was allowed to hold in common another 30,000 acres

After their reservation was divided into tracts of land, the Nez Perce received 80 acres per person and the "surplus" land was sold to the U.S. government. A group of Nez Perce men and bank officials pose in front of a table covered in coins and bills in this 1895 image. *(University of Washington)*

Tribes such as the Nez Perce, who were not accustomed to farming, often had difficulty adjusting to an agricultural lifestyle and would instead lease the land they received through Allotment. Louie Pierre poses, gripping the handle of a hoe, for this 1914 portrait taken during the Flathead Irrigation Project. *(National Archives and Records Administration)*

of range and timberlands. That left 542,064 acres of surplus land. The tribal leaders did not want to sell the surplus to the government, but they were given no choice. The U.S. government gave the tribe $3.00 an acre for the rest of the land. One million dollars was put in a trust fund for the tribe while the balance was distributed directly to tribe members who each received approximately $600.

The Nez Perce and the other Plateau tribes had never been farmers and had little or no interest in starting farms. Restrictions on the transfer allotments also created problems. Original owners of an allotment were not allowed to sell their land nor could they deed it to an individual. When someone died, their allotment was divided up among all their relatives. Many Indians who did not want to farm their allotments leased them to white farmers and tried to live on the small rents they received from their land.

Allotment was disastrous for most of the Plateau tribes in the United States. In British Columbia, Canada, though, the Indians were in some ways treated worse as the province just took most of the good land without consideration for any claims the Indians had. A commission was established to oversee the settlement of Indians on reserves (the Canadian equivalent of a reservation), allotting land to individuals and bands but mostly ensuring that the best lands went to white settlers.

As the 19th century came to a close, the outlook for Plateau Indians was not good. Loss of land destroyed any chance people had of anything resembling a traditional lifestyle. Most of the Plateau Indians, on both sides of the U.S.-Canadian border, became some of the poorest people in the region. It would be many decades before hope for better treatment was revived for the Plateau Indians.

7

Plateau Indians in the Twentieth Century

As the 20th century began, the situation for Plateau Indians seemed bleak. It appeared that the underlying aim of the Dawes Act to eventually eliminate all Native American tribes was going to come true. In 1906, the Burke Act amended the Dawes Act. The Burke Act made it possible for individuals to sell their allotments. This started another land rush by unscrupulous land speculators and individuals to buy up much of the allotted land. Without their allotted lands, many Plateau Indians became extremely poor. Even when the government attempted to help them, the result was often of little benefit or even harmful.

Indian children were sometimes sent to schools where they were forced to convert to Christianity and were taught that much of their traditional culture was inferior to that of mainstream U.S. society. A group of boys kneel and pray before bedtime at St. Mary's Mission School in Omak, Washington. *(University of Washington)*

EDUCATION

In the latter days of the 19th century, numerous church groups became involved on the reservations of the Plateau. This was seen by many whites as a way to eliminate some of the corruption that plagued the running of the reservations. However, the missionaries sent to the reservations became strong agents

Spokane Indian students at Fort Spokane, Washington, pose for a 1904 portrait. The formal dresses and hats or bonnets for women and suits for men were an attempt to assimilate Indian children into mainstream U.S. culture. *(University of Washington Libraries, Special Collections, NA 4118)*

for the assimilation of the people they were sent to help. Attempts were made to convert all Indians to Christianity. Children were often forced to attend school. Many were taken from their families and sent to boarding schools on and off the reservations. In these schools, children were taught that their Indian ways were wrong. They were forced to wear uniforms or other non-Indian clothing. In addition, most schools forbade the use of any language except English.

Many of the schools presented programs that were intended to teach students a trade. Often these included skills that were of no use on the reservation. Some schools had work projects that exploited the labor of the children. Many children who attended these schools found themselves losing their Indian identity but they were unable to become members of the white community as Indians did not even become U.S. citizens until 1924. At this time, Congress passed the Citizenship Act granting all Indians citizenship. This was done in part because so many American Indians had joined the military during World War I.

WATER RIGHTS

Farming in the arid regions of the Plateau was a difficult task without the aid of irrigation. In 1908, the U.S. Supreme Court ruled in the case of *Winters v. United States* that Indians living on land that had been part of reservations had priority over the use of water in the rivers in their areas. However, moving the water from the rivers to the fields required dams, canals, and other improvements that the Indians did not have the resources to build.

During the early 1900s, the U.S. government created numerous irrigation programs in order to pipe water to reservations, but these programs were often abandoned. A few structures on arid land mark the remnants of the Flathead Irrigation Project in this photograph ca. 1948 to 1952. *(National Archives and Records Administration)*

Plateau and other American Indians looked to the federal government to assist them in creating irrigation projects. Projects were planned on the Yakama, Flathead, and Klamath reservations. These and other projects took many years to complete and often the water traveled first to white farmers on and around the reservation areas. The Flathead project is a prime example of how the Indians once again were shortchanged by the U.S. government. When completed, the project provided irrigation for almost 126,000 acres. However, by the late 20th century, only about 15,000 of those irrigated acres still belonged to Indians.

The Indian Reorganization Act of 1934 sought to reinstate self-government by American Indian tribes. In this photograph from May 11, 1934, a delegation of Yakama Indians led by Chief Saluskin poses on the steps of the Capitol building in Washington, D.C., prior to a hearing about the bill. *(Library of Congress, Prints and Photographs Division [LC-DIG-ppmsca-05078])*

A NEW DEAL FOR THE PLATEAU INDIANS

In 1929, the United States and the rest of the world were plunged into the Great Depression. This was a time of financial hardship for everyone from the U.S. government and the largest businesses to most individuals. What little help the Indians of the Plateau had been getting all but came to an end. However, in 1932 newly elected president Franklin D. Roosevelt promised a "New Deal" for all people in the country. During his administration, the U.S. government began numerous public works projects and created new policies designed to put people back to work. For many, the American Indians had been forgotten on their isolated reservations. Roosevelt and those around him wanted to include them in their vision for the future of the country.

Roosevelt appointed John Collier as the commissioner of Indian Affairs. Collier had founded the American Indian Defense Associ-

AMERICAN INDIAN DEFENSE ASSOCIATION

In 1923, social worker John Collier formed the American Indian Defense Association with the aid of numerous white people who shared a sense of compassion for American Indians. For 10 years, Collier served as the executive secretary of the organization. By 1932, the organization had 1,700 members who supported the efforts of Collier and his staff. They lobbied the U.S. Congress on Indian rights issues as well as directly supporting tribes that were trying to fight the government on a wide variety of issues.

Beginning in 1925, AIDA began publishing *American Indian Life,* a newsletter about Indian issues that frequently criticized the government's policies. After Collier moved on to work for the Bureau of Indian Affairs (BIA) in 1936, AIDA merged with another Indian advocacy group to form the Association of American Indian Affairs, which continues to work for Indian rights today.

ation (AIDA) and had been a champion for Indian rights. Collier spearheaded a new direction for Indians across the country. The ideas of assimilation and allotment were soon reversed under the Indian Reorganization Act of 1934.

Under the Indian Reorganization Act, the policy of allotting Indian land officially came to an end. Any surplus land that had not been sold was returned to the tribes. Even more important to the survival of Indian tribes was the provision that encouraged tribes to organize their own governments and write tribal constitutions. Once tribes did this, they were able to take over many of the tasks formerly handled by outsiders who worked for the BIA. Those BIA employees who remained were put under civil service regulations, and Collier encouraged his agency to hire Indians whenever possible.

On the Plateau, the Flathead were the first to take advantage of the Indian Reorganization Act. They quickly wrote and adopted a tribal constitution and set up their own government in 1935. The following year, they created a tribal corporation to manage the almost 200,000 acres they got back from the U.S. government. They leased some of the rangeland and began harvesting timber to benefit the tribe as a whole. They used some of this money to buy back allotments that had been sold to non-Indians. They soon had their own sawmill, which provided a number of jobs for tribal members.

The New Deal also provided help to the Indians of the Plateau through some of its programs that were directed toward all U.S. citizens. The Civilian Conservation Corps (CCC) gave young

In 1936, the Flathead (Salish) created a tribal corporation to manage the money they received from the U.S. government as a result of the Indian Reorganization Act. In this 1937 photograph, a group of Flathead men, surrounded by tipis, gathered around a drum. *(Library of Congress, Prints and Photographs Division [LC-USZ62-115460])*

people jobs working on numerous public projects, and it created an Indian division. The projects this division of CCC undertook primarily involved making improvements to timberlands on the reservations. Roads were built to make remote forest areas more accessible. Fire towers were erected and other work was done to protect and improve forest land. Other projects began to improve rangeland.

WORLD WAR II

On December 7, 1941, Japanese forces attacked Pearl Harbor, Hawaii, drawing the United States into World War II; the entire country changed almost overnight. Many of the progressive social programs of Roosevelt and his administration came to an end as resources and manpower were channeled into the war effort. Many American Indians from the Plateau and around the country joined the military as they had done in

World War I. Those who stayed home often found jobs supporting the war effort.

When the war ended in 1945, many soldiers, Indian and non-Indian, returned home with the idea that they wanted a different life for themselves and their families. Many moved to urban areas in hopes of finding better paying jobs in industry. Those American Indians who returned home to their reservations wanted to improve conditions for themselves, their families, and their tribes.

The activism that had started in the period between the two world wars became the focus for many Indians around the country. In addition, many in the U.S. government had once again changed their ideas about how to deal with what they saw as the problem of the American Indian. New policies attempted to put an end to the American Indians as a separate group within the United States.

TERMINATION

The years following World War II are often referred to as the cold war as the U.S. government was locked in a struggle for social and political influence around the world with the communist government of the Soviet Union. Many feared that communist ideas would spread to the United States and threaten the American way of life. As fear grew, many became suspicious of anything that appeared to endorse the communist concepts of communal ownership of property and collective government.

The attitude in Washington, D.C., became one of terminating or eliminating Indian tribes around the nation. Between 1954 and 1962, Congress terminated the government's relationship with 61 tribes. Among the tribes of the American Plateau only the Klamath were terminated; they were one of the first in 1945. The members of the Klamath tribe agreed to be terminated as a tribe in exchange for a division of tribal assets. At the time, they gave up a reservation of more than 1,000,000 acres. Life had never been easy on reservations in the Plateau region or anywhere else for that matter. As a terminated tribe, the Klamath lost what little support they had received from the government. Many among the Klamath quickly realized that they had made a terrible mistake and began to petition the government for reinstatement of their tribal rights.

During this time, the Indian Claims Commission (ICC) settled two cases in favor of the Klamath. Both involved compensation for lands lost. In 1964, the commission awarded $2.5 million, plus an additional $4.2 million in 1969. Despite the fact that the commission still recognized the rights of the tribe under the treaty it had agreed to in 1864, it took until 1986 before the Klamath regained its status as a federally recognized tribe.

As part of the effort to end the separate identity of American Indians, in 1952 Congress created the Voluntary Relocation Program. This program provided help to Indians who wanted to leave the reservation and move to urban areas. Although many Indians tried to take advantage of the program, it often fell short of its stated goals. Once they moved, little help was

After World War II, the U.S. government's policy toward the American Indian population was one that proposed Termination and appropriation of tribal lands. A boarded-up church is the remnant of an Indian fishing village along the Columbia River in Washington State as depicted in this 1970 photograph. *(National Archives and Records Administration)*

INDIAN CLAIMS COMMISSION

The Indian Claims Commission was established in 1946 to handle the many land claims brought against the U.S. government by numerous Indian tribes. Most of these cases involved the loss of land and other benefits promised under treaties made with the government. The ICC heard more than 300 cases and awarded $800 million to tribes for land lost in violation of treaties. When possible, they also returned federal land to the tribes. The Yakama, for example, got back 21,000 acres in 1972. The ICC operated until 1978.

As a result of the Indian Claims Commission, in 1972 the Yakama recovered 21,000 acres of land that had been stolen from the tribe. A group of Yakama Indians protect the entrance of the Yakama Indian Reservation in Washington State in this photograph from the 1950s. *(University of Washington Libraries, Special Collections, NA 761)*

provided and many Indians joined other ethnic minorities living in urban poverty.

FIGHTING FOR FISH

Most of the treaties agreed to by the Plateau tribes included their right to continue to hunt and fish at their traditional sites. However, these rights were often denied them shortly after or even before the treaties were ratified. Reservation property rarely

The Grand Coulee Dam, pictured here, was constructed along the Columbia River in central Washington State in 1941 to provide hydroelectric power to the city of Spokane, which is 100 miles to the south. However, flooding caused by the dam displaced thousands of American Indians who lived on nearby Colville Reservation. *(AP Images)*

included the best land along the rivers of the Plateau region, and conflicts began in the 19th century, especially over who could fish where. When non-Indian settlers began arriving on the Plateau, they almost immediately began to take advantage of the large salmon runs.

By the 1870s, a commercial fishing industry was well established. Fish wheels that could harvest huge quantities of salmon were constructed at some of the best traditional Indian fishing sites along the Columbia River. In the 20th century, numerous court cases arose as Indians were excluded from fishing sites or because of attempts by the states to regulate Indian fishing. Many of these cases eventually made it to the U.S. Supreme Court. In case after case, the Court overturned the state courts and found in favor of Indian fishing rights guaranteed in numerous treaties.

Further assaults to Indian fishing traditions came about in the 20th century when the government began building dams on many of the Plateau rivers. Both the Bonneville and Grand Coulee Dams on the Columbia River, which were begun in the 1930s, caused losses to the Indians of the Plateau. Bonneville Dam, located near the border of Washington and Oregon, includes a fish ladder to allow salmon and steelhead to swim above the dam. However, the lake behind the dam caused the loss of many traditional fishing sites.

Grand Coulee Dam is located in central Washington on the upper Columbia River. No fish ladder was included with the dam, which meant that salmon and other fish could no longer reach Indian fishing sites on the upper river. The lake behind Grand Coulee covers hundreds of square miles and is more than 200 miles long. Some of the land that is under the lake was part of the Colville Reservation. The Bureau of Reclamation, which was in charge of the dam project, failed to settle the land claims of the tribe and individual allottees. In 1940, Indians on the reservation were forced out of their homes by the rising water behind the dam.

The Indian agent on the reservation sent desperate telegrams to President Roosevelt about the losses to the reservation. Finally, on June 29, 1940, Congress approved a plan to compensate the Indians who had lost their homes and land. They also promised that 25 percent of the lake would be available for use by the people of the reservation.

Located between the states of Washington and Oregon, the rapids at Celilo Falls had been one of the most important Indian fishing sites for thousands of years. When the government proposed a dam at The Dalles, which would inundate the falls, they settled all fishing claims before they began construction. The loss of this fishing site and increasing conflict with commercial and sport fishing groups led to further court cases.

In 1968, David and Richard Sohappy of the Yakama tribe were arrested by state authorities for using a gill net. This was a

FISH-INS

In the 1960s, there were many protests around the United States. African Americans were fighting for their civil rights, and many people were protesting against the war in Vietnam. Although American Indians had been actively fighting for their rights for many years, many became more active during the 1960s.

In 1964, the National Indian Youth Council organized a protest along the Columbia River against the loss of traditional fishing rights by many tribes of the Plateau Region. The event was called a fish-in, and representatives of a number of tribes gathered on the river to fish for salmon in defiance of state regulations. Their goal was to make non-Indians aware that for them fishing was a part of their traditional way of life. They also wanted to make people aware of how the state and federal government had ignored rights granted to the Indians by treaty. This form of civil disobedience has since become a useful tactic on the Plateau on a number of occasions.

traditional way of fishing but was not allowed by state regulations. Before the case was settled, the Nez Perce, Warm Springs, Umatilla, and Yakama tribes all became involved. In 1969, a federal judge ordered that the state of Oregon had to ensure that the Indians in the state had the opportunity to harvest a fair share of the salmon that run in the state's rivers. The judge also suggested that there needed to be more cooperation between all parties that had an interest in the fishery. This included commercial and sport fisherman, federal and state authorities, as well as the tribes.

Partially as a result of this and also because the tribes had received money in a number of fishing rights and land claim cases, the four tribes that were involved in the Sohappy case formed the Columbia River Inter-Tribal Fish Commission in 1977. The commission continues to this day and is involved in all aspects of the salmon fishery in the Columbia River basin. They have worked on habitat management and improvement, fish passages, site access issues, and numerous research studies. The commission is also an advocate for Indian fishing rights and a protector of the resource so that the Indians of the Plateau will continue to have access to this traditional resource for generations to come.

ELIZABETH WOODY
(1959–   )

Fish-ins and other forms of protest have been one way some people have expressed their dissatisfaction with the treatment of the Indians of the Plateau by the U.S. government. Some tribal leaders had the foresight to form the Columbia River Inter-Tribal Fish Commission to try and improve fishing and help their people receive their fair share of the harvestable fish in the river. Others have their own unique ways of bringing atten-

tion to the problems of Indian rights. Elizabeth Woody is an activist who has tried to help her people through poetry and other forms of art.

Woody is of mixed Indian heritage with ancestors belonging to the Navajo, Warm Springs, Wasco, and Yakama tribes. She is an enrolled member of the Confederated Tribes of Warm Springs and has spent much of her life in Oregon. Woody is a well-known writer whose poetry often discusses the problems facing her people. She has been outspoken about the mistreatment of American Indians by the federal government especially in the area of treaty rights. She has been most concerned with the loss of fishing rights as it is a central part of the culture of her people and as they continue to be lost due to regulations and dams.

Woody has received many awards, including an American Book Award from the American Booksellers Association for *Hand Into Stone*, for her poetry and photography and has had three books published. She is also active in a number of organizations that encourage American Indian writers and artists. She currently works for Ecotrust, an environmental advocacy group in Portland, Oregon, that is trying to help restore the environment of the Pacific Northwest and Alaska so that it can once again support the vast quantities of salmon and other animals of the past.

Elizabeth Woody, pictured here, is a writer and poet who has spent most of her life in Oregon. She focuses on the mistreatment of American Indians by the U.S. government—especially the loss of traditional rights, such as that of fishing. *(By Joe Cantrell)*

BOOKS BY ELIZABETH WOODY

Hand into Stone. New York: Contact II Publications, 1988.

Luminaries of the Humble. Tucson: University of Arizona Press, 1994.

Seven Hands, Seven Hearts. Portland, Ore.: Eighth Mountain Press, 1994.

In the Canadian part of the Plateau, there have also been a number of conflicts over hunting and fishing rights for Indians. After numerous court cases reaffirmed the rights of what Canadians call First Nations, the British Columbia Claims Task Force was created in 1990. The purpose of this organization was to create a framework to negotiate settlements with the Indians rather than have the courts decide on these cases. The creation of the task force set the stage for new treaties that would compensate the First Nations for land and other rights lost unfairly in the past. The negotiations are an ongoing process that has both sides optimistic that they will come to a fair settlement for the Indians of British Columbia.

8

The Indians of the Plateau Today

Life of the Plateau Indians today is often difficult from an economic and health perspective. At the same time, many of today's Indians in the region have expressed a renewed interest in their languages and traditional beliefs and activities. Many tribes continue to benefit from economic development that resulted from land claims during the 20th century. Resorts and now casinos provide jobs and income for some of the tribes in the region while others profit from natural resources such as timber.

TRIBAL ENTERPRISES

Although many Indian communities in the Plateau region fall economically behind the non-Indian population, in the early years of the 21st century numerous tribal enterprises were prospering and helping their people. Some of these enterprises began in the middle of the 20th century when many of the southern Plateau tribes received large cash settlements from the U.S. government. These payments were the result of land and fishing rights claims and often amounted to millions of dollars for the tribes. Many tribal members wanted these settlements to be divided immediately among the members of the tribe in equal shares. Some of the money was distributed in this way but was quickly spent by most of the recipients. Much of the money was used by the tribes to fund numerous projects that would have lasting benefit to the tribe.

Money was spent to provide services that most non-Indians took for granted. Wells were dug to provide individual houses with running water. Septic systems were installed to allow for indoor plumbing. Other projects were begun to benefit larger groups or entire tribes. Community centers were built in a number of locations that gave tribal members a place to gather. The Nez Perce and others set some of the money aside to provide scholarships to help educate the young people of the tribe.

In 1946, the Salish and Kootenai took $550,000 and invested it in the construction of the Flathead Hot Springs Resort and were the first Plateau tribes to take advantage of the growing interest in tourism in the region. The Confederated Tribes of Warm Springs spent some of the money they received as compensation for the loss of fishing at Celilo Falls in the development of their own resort. The Kah-nee-ta Hot Springs opened on Memorial Day, 1964, with a hotel, lodge, and campground plus the featured hot springs. These are piped into a series of pools. The first maintains a temperature of 123°F and then flows into a large swimming pool where the water temperature is 80°F. Since opening, the Warm Springs resort has added a golf course and other amenities. In the 1990s, they have also opened the Indian Head Gaming Center which has added casino gambling to the resort.

Many other tribes invested their money wisely as well. Tribes, such as the Confederated Tribes of the Yakama Reservation, took over the management of their own forest resources and have built successful tribal businesses that include timber harvesting as well as wood processing, although by 2005 the Yakama wood products business was experiencing problems as the national housing boom slowed. Many tribes have built their own sawmills. Improvements have also been made in the areas of farming and stock raising. Some, like the Spokane, have benefited from the discovery of various mineral deposits on their land. Uranium mines on the Spokane reservation have provided that tribe with a steady income.

Some tribes around the country have found work providing outsourced labor for government agencies that cannot ship work overseas. In 2006, the Umatilla-owned Cayuse Technologies Company signed an agreement with the national company Accenture Limited. The partnership between the two companies may eventually employ 250 people on the Umatilla Reservation who will perform data entry and other tasks under federal government contracts.

In recent years, basketball has become a popular sport on many reservations in the United States. Yakama Nation Tribal Council Secretary Davis Washines announces the tribe's purchase of the Yakama Sun Kings during a news conference at Legends Casino in Toppenish, Washington, on June 23, 2005. *(AP Images/Jeff Haller)*

In a move that surprised many and angered some tribal members, the Yakama tribe in 2005 purchased the minor league basketball team known as the Sun Kings that play in nearby Yakima. Basketball is one of the most popular sports among Indians on reservations around the country. Tribal involvement with the Sun Kings has heightened interest in the team and seems to be encouraging interest around the country in American Indian basketball players. Right now there is only one Indian, Richard Dionne (Sioux), playing at the professional level, and the Sun Kings brought him to their team shortly after the Yakama tribe became its owners.

In the Plateau region, water rights have long been an obstacle to tribal development. Many tribes were cheated out of their rights to water from the region's rivers by non-Indian politicians who supported white ranchers and farmers. In 2005, the state of Idaho finally settled a long standing dispute with the Nez Perce tribe. In the settlement, the Nez Perce got a 30-year contract that guarantees them 50,000 acre-feet of water from the Snake River. In addition, the tribe received a cash settlement of $193 million and additional land for their reservation. This settlement gives the tribe the water and resources to go forward with agricultural development on the reservation.

The tribes have also pooled their wealth to support organizations such as the Columbia River Inter-Tribal Fish Commission. Even more important has been the Affiliated Tribes of the Northwest Indians, which was formed in 1953 to further issues that confront the Indian people of the Northwest. Today, the organization represents 54 tribes in the Plateau region as well as tribes from the Northwest coast and southeast Alaska. From its headquarters in Portland, Oregon, the group gives technical support to tribes in a number of ways including economic development. In addition, they provide a unified voice for the tribes they represent when publicizing problems or programs that affect the Indians of the region.

CASINOS

One area of economic development that has been met with a certain amount of resistance from both Indians and non-Indians has been Indian casinos and other types of gambling enterprises. Including casinos operated by the coastal tribes of Washington, Oregon, and Idaho, there are 31 Indian casinos in the three states. The casinos range in size from very small to huge depending on the proximity to large populations of potential gamblers. The It'se-Ye-Ye Casino operated by the Nez Perce in Kamiah, Idaho, is only 6,000 square feet and has 100 slot machines. The Tulalip Casino operated by the coastal Tulalip tribe is only 30 minutes from Seattle and is 227,000 square feet in size. This casino has 1,000 slot machines, 49 table games like blackjack and poker, plus an 850-seat bingo room.

There is no doubt that the revenue generated by casinos has helped tribes in the Plateau region. However, they are also causing friction between the tribes, who are often competing for the same gamblers. In Oregon, the state has attempted to limit tribes to one casino per reservation. This has allowed the

The establishment of casinos on reservations has proved controversial among both American Indians and non-American Indians. David J. Matheson, chief executive officer of gaming for the Coeur d'Alene, stands in front of a sign for a casino in Worley, Idaho. *(AP Images/Jeff T. Green)*

Grande Ronde Indian Head Casino near Portland to generate annual profits of $76 million, while the Confederated Tribes of Warm Springs only make around $4 million from their casino.

The Warm Springs tribes want to build a new casino on land they own near the Hood River which would situate them much closer to the population centered around Portland. The Warm Springs tribe has projected that they could net $14 or $15 million annually at the Hood River location. The state

NEZ PERCE BUY BACK ARTIFACTS

In 1846, missionary Henry Spalding reportedly paid $57.90 for a number of Nez Perce-made goods including tools, clothing, a cradleboard, and other everyday items. When Spalding left Idaho, he returned to his native Ohio and donated his collection of artifacts to Oberlin College in 1893. The 20 items were later passed on to the Ohio Historical Society.

In 1979, the society lent some of the items to the Nez Perce to display in the Nez Perce National Historical Park near Lewiston, Idaho. In 1995, the society gave the Nez Perce a choice: They could return the items or buy the entire collection for its appraised value of $608,100. Many thought that this was outrageous; however, the society stood firm. The Nez Perce did not have the money to buy back the items and were faced with losing these important cultural items. When news of the situation spread, a campaign was begun to raise the money for the items.

Lillian Disney, the wife of the late animator and theme park creator Walt Disney, donated $100,000 and the tribe received more than 4,000 smaller donations. Many of the donations totaling more than $40,000 came from schoolchildren, including $2,500 from an elementary school in Boise, Idaho. Other donors included the band Pearl Jam and the Potlatch Corporation. Eventually, the entire amount was raised and the Nez Perce now own these important items from their past to share with all who visit their homelands.

has resisted breaking its one casino per reservation rule and the Grande Ronde Indians are siding with the state. They fear that once the gate is opened to the Warm Springs tribes, other groups will attempt to site casinos near Portland and take away their business.

Despite the disparity of income between the casinos, many tribes have benefited in jobs and income from their gaming establishments. Although some people disapprove of gambling establishments, there is no doubt that Indian gaming has provided a great boost for Indians on the Plateau and throughout the country. Much of the money has been used for educational and cultural programs that have benefited many tribal members.

CULTURAL REVIVAL

Despite all the efforts by the federal government at Assimilation, Allotment, Termination, and Relocation, most tribes have fought to hold onto many aspects of their traditional culture. In fact, many Plateau tribes are using their resources achieved from gaming and other tribal enterprises to preserve and promote their culture. Cultural centers that celebrate and preserve Indian heritage have been built on many reservations in the region. These centers have served as a depository for cultural materials from the past. In some instances, materials collected by non-Indians have been returned to the tribes.

Many tribes have also started projects to teach and preserve their original languages. Some Indian languages of the

Fred Hill, Jr., a teacher at Nixyaawii Charter School, instructs a class in learning the Sahaptian (Penutian) language on the Umatilla Indian Reservation in December 2004. Such classes bring tribal elders and youths together in an attempt to preserve the tribe's language and culture. *(AP Images/Don Ryan)*

Voting by the American Indian population reached record highs during the 2004 U.S. presidential election. Buttons advocating voting are arranged on the Native American Law Students Association's table during the 2004 Indian Law Conference trade fair in Albuquerque, New Mexico, on April 15, 2004. *(AP Images/Jake Schoellkopf)*

Plateau such as Cayuse have already been lost and others were on the verge of extinction. The programs vary on the different reservations of the region but most are doing something. The state of Oregon even passed a bill to help promote the teaching of Native languages. On the reservation of the Confederated Tribes of Umatilla, the language office is a casual place set up more like a lounge than a classroom. Elders of the tribe come there and get a cup of coffee and make themselves available to a linguist who is working to preserve their languages. At the same time, young people from the tribe stop by to ask language questions or hear stories told in their own language.

The Warm Springs Reservation children have their Native language included in the curriculum of their school. Starting as early as kindergarten, the 300 students in the elementary school spend about half an hour a day, four days a week, learning their language. Many feel that children who have increased pride in their heritage from learning the language of their ancestors will have a better chance of staying in school and succeeding in life.

Powwows have also become important to Plateau Indians and Indians elsewhere in North America. At a powwow, Indians from many tribes gather to socialize and perform traditional dances. The costumes they wear often include elements created by traditional means. Another tradition that has been maintained by Plateau powwows is playing the stick game. Powwows also provide an opportunity for Indians to meet and discuss other issues.

Prior to the U.S. presidential election in 2004, there was a national effort to get more Indians to vote. In 2000, the Indian vote had helped defeat Senator Slade Gorton of Washington State who was an open opponent of Indian rights in the Northwest. In addition, a higher percentage of Indian voters participated in other 2000 national and local elections than in previous ones; many activists hoped that in 2004 even more Indians would go to the polls. In Washington State, where there are more than 100,000 American Indian and Alaskan Native voters, a rally was held at the Iwasil Powwow in October 2004. Local and national Indian leaders attended the powwow and the accompanying Native Vote 2004 Rally. Turnout of Indian voters in the Northwest and around the country reached new highs in the 2004 elections.

INDIANS OF THE PLATEAU TODAY

For Plateau Indians, the future looks brighter today than it has since non-Indians first arrived in the region more than 200 years ago. Casinos and other tribal enterprises have provided more economic opportunities than existed in the past. Cultural revival among the tribes has given many Indians a stronger connection to their ethnic identity. Protests, lawsuits, and a number

DEVIL'S CLUB

In the first half of the 20th century, white doctors in British Columbia learned that Indians in the region were using a tea made from the roots of the plant known as devil's club (*Echinopanax horridum*) to control the symptoms of type II diabetes. Research showed that the herbal remedy acts like insulin to help regulate the blood sugar levels in users. It is likely that devil's club had been a part of the Indian herbal medicine chest for a very long time. It was not until the 1940s that non-Indian scientists began research into the use of plant-based medication for the treatment of the disease. In the 1960s, this type of drug became a regular part of treatment for type II diabetes.

Devil's club is now being marketed by Indians and Alaskan Natives as an herbal remedy. This tall, broadleaf bush has large thorns on both the leaves and stems and grows wild in almost impenetrable thickets in low, wet areas from Alaska south to California.

of Indian organizations have helped recapture many Indian rights that had been promised by treaties but lost in the late 19th and early 20th centuries.

However, Indians on the Plateau have not yet become the economic equals of non-Indians of the region. One area of concern for American Indians is related to the increased incidence of type II diabetes. Among Indians who are 55 to 64 years old, a 2002 study indicated that 30 percent of American Indians and Alaskan Natives have type II diabetes. Within the same age group in the general population of the United States, the incidence of type II diabetes is less than 14 percent.

The higher percentage of cases of type II diabetes in American Indians is caused in part by a genetic predilection to the disease and in part by lifestyle issues including obesity and inactivity. However, there is hope for the future. The Indian Health Care Improvement Act (IHCIA), first passed by the U.S. Congress in 1976 and amended and updated in 1988, 1992, 1996, and 2000, provides for a number of programs aimed at handling the problems of type II diabetes and other Indian health issues. In fall 2005, the IHCIA was again expected to be reauthorized by Congress. In the area of diabetes, model treatment plans were funded at the Bellingham Health Center in Washington State and at various sites in Oregon. In part because

Tribes of the U.S. Plateau, 2000	
Plateau Tribes	**2000 Census**
Coeur d'Alene	1523
Colville	8398
Kalispel	228
Klamath	2734
Kootenai	2734
Modoc	573
Nez Perce	4082
Salish	3500
Salish-Kootenai (Flathead)	3385
Spokane	2446
Umatilla	1608
Warm Springs	3190
Yakama	8337

Note: Total American Indian population is 42,738. Figures are from the 2000 census.

Source: U.S. Census Bureau, 2000 Census of Population and Housing, Characteristics of American Indians and Alaska Natives by tribe and Language: 2000, PHC-5, Washington, D.C., 20030.

Every 10 years the United States conducts a national census of the people living in the country. According to the most recent census, there are almost 43,000 members of Plateau tribes living in the United States.

of these programs, American Indians in the Northwest have the lowest incidence of type II diabetes among Indians around the country.

The IHCIA also addresses other health problems that confront American Indians. Among them are alcoholism and other substance abuse issues. American Indians and Alaskan Natives have a genetic predisposition to alcoholism. This has been an ongoing problem among Indian groups throughout the country ever since the first European offered alcohol in exchange for furs and other trade goods. Many Plateau tribes have initiated programs to help prevent alcohol and other substance abuse related problems. They are also working to help tribal members who are already experiencing difficulties. Progress is also being made in other areas.

According to the 2000 U.S. Census, there are 42,738 members of Plateau tribes in the United States. A number of the tribes that existed at the beginning of the historical period are no longer recognized. For instance, the Cayuse, Walla Walla, and the Umatilla agreed to join together on the Umatilla Reservation in the treaty of 1855. In 2000, the census listed 1,608 people who claim to be Umatilla but does not report any Walla Walla or Cayuse. The same is true of the 3,190 people reported as belonging to the Confederated Tribes of Warm Springs. A number of small tribes that lived along the lower reaches of the Columbia River were forced together on the Warm Springs Reservation and through intermarriage and governmental practices have come to be seen as one tribe.

The largest reported group of Plateau Indians in the United States is the Colville. Historically, the Colville were a unique group that lived on both sides of the U.S.-Canada border along the upper Columbia River. In 1872, the Colville Reservation was established in Washington State, and other groups were forced to join the Colville. Today, the descendents of those people are all considered Colville by the U.S. Census and make up the largest Plateau group with 8,398 members. The Yakama with 8,337 members are very close. They are also in a similar situation in which members of other tribes that settled on their reservation in the 19th century are now all counted together.

In Canada, it is more difficult to find population statistics that count individual tribes, or bands as they are called there. In British Columbia, there were 3,868,875 total people living in the province in 2001. Of that number, 170,025 reported that they belonged to an aboriginal (Native) group. In Canada, they refer to the Native Americans as First Nations and separate out any people who are part Indian and part non-Indian as Métis as well as those who are members of Inuit bands. The number of people who are considered North American Indians living in British Columbia, including both Plateau and Coastal groups, is 118,295. This number most likely includes a number of Indians who are not native to British Columbia but have moved to Vancouver, the largest Canadian city on the Pacific coast.

Despite the advances that Plateau Indians have made in recent years, many of them still live below the poverty level. Among the total U.S. population, the 2000 census reported that 12.4 percent lived below the poverty level. At the same time, the percentage of American Indians living in the United States below the poverty level was double that at 25.7 percent. Among U.S. Plateau Indians, the Modoc at 40.5 percent, the Warm Springs at 33.2 percent, and the Yakama at 32 percent were the worst off economically. Most of the other tribes were close to the percentage of all American Indians. Only the Umatilla at 17.9 percent living below the poverty level were substantially better off than American Indians as a whole.

Further economic development on the reservations of the Plateau as well as social and health programs give many American Indians of the Plateau an optimistic outlook for the future. Despite repeated attempts by the U.S. and Canadian governments to eliminate all Indians, the Plateau tribes have survived. They are finding the balance needed to be both American Indians and members of the Canadian and U.S. systems. Many hope that they and future generations will be able to maintain their unique identity while becoming economically, legally, and politically equal to non-Indians throughout North America.

⧊ Time Line ⧊

⁂ **9000 to 6000** B.C.

The people of the Plateau live in small nomadic bands during the Early Period.

⁂ **6000 to 2000** B.C.

During this period of transition, the climate of the Plateau becomes cooler, enabling the salmon to swim further upriver.

⁂ **2000** B.C. **to** A.D. **1720**

With the increased fish, people of the Plateau tend to live in larger villages of 100 houses or more.

⁂ **400** B.C. **to** A.D. **500**

The use of the bow and arrow becomes widespread in the area.

⁂ A.D. **1000**

By A.D. 1000, the people of the Plateau have divided into the tribes that will exist at their first contact with Europeans.

⁂ **Late 1600s to early 1700s**

The horse is first introduced to the Plateau region.

⁂ **1780**

A smallpox epidemic sweeps through the Plateau, killing thousands.

⁂ **1793**

Alexander MacKenzie, a Scottish fur trader and explorer, was the first European north of Mexico to reach the Pacific Ocean on an overland route in 1793.

1805

Captain Meriwether Lewis and Lieutenant William Clark explore the Plateau, with Shoshone Sacajawea as their guide.

1807

The North West Company establish their first trading post among the Kootenai in the northern Plateau region.

1811

The North West Company opens a trading post near the mouth of the Columbia River at Fort Astoria, in present-day Oregon.

1842

Doctor Elijah White leads a group of white settlers to Oregon City, Oregon.

1846

The United States and Britain reach an agreement on conflicting claims in the Plateau region.

1853

The U.S. Congress creates Washington Territory.

1877

The Nez Perce War is fought.

1887

The U.S. Congress passed the General Allotment, or Dawes Act, to parcel out land to individual Indians.

1906

Congress passes the Burke Act, allowing individual Indians to sell their allotments.

1908

The U.S. Supreme Court sides with American Indians in *Winters v. United States* on water rights.

1934

The Indian Reorganization Act is passed, ending the policy of allotting Indian land and encouraging tribes to organize.

1935

Following passage of the Indian Reorganization Act, the Flathead draft and pass a tribal constitution and set up their own government.

1945

The Klamath are terminated as a tribe.

1946

The Salish and Kootenai invest $550,000 in the construction of the Flathead Hot Springs Resort.

1953

The Affiliated Tribes of the Northwest, a group that fosters fighting for equal rights for Northwest Indians, is founded.

1964

The National Indian Youth Council organizes a protest along the Columbia River to protest the loss of traditional fishing rights by many tribes of the Plateau.

The Confederated Tribes of Warm Springs open the Kah-nee-ta Hot Springs resort.

1968

David and Richard Sohappy are arrested for using a gill net to catch fish; various Yakama countersue.

1969

A judge orders the state of Oregon to ensure Indians have a fair share of the salmon runs in the state.

1972

The Yakama regain 20,000 acres as part of a land claims case.

1977

The Columbia River Inter-Tribal Fish Commission is founded.

1986

The Klamath regain their tribal status from the U.S. government.

1995

The Nez Perce raise the money needed to buy their own artifacts from the Ohio Historical Society.

2000

American Indians in Washington State vote in record numbers to defeat Senator Slade Gorton, an opponent of Indian rights.

2004

The Native Vote 2004 Rally is held in Washington State to encourage American Indians to vote in the 2004 elections.

🏹 2005

Against the wishes of a number of tribes, the 9,000-year-old skeleton called Kennewick Man, found on the banks of the Columbia River, is examined by anthropologists at the University of Washington.

Idaho and the Nez Perce Tribe settle their long-standing water rights dispute.

The Yakama Tribe purchase the Sun Kings, a minor league basketball team based in Yakima, Washington.

🏹 2006

The Umatilla-owned Cayuse Technology Company enters an agreement with Accenture Ltd. to bring outsourced data entry jobs on government contracts to the reservation.

🏹 2007

September 29—The 11th annual Nez Perce Art in the Wallowa show celebrates traditional contemporary Native American art from Plateau artists.

🏹 2008

January 26—Yakama woman Elyse Umemoto places as second runner-up in Miss America pageant.

Historical Sites
and Museums

Idaho

POCATELLO

Idaho Museum of Natural History   The museum has extensive collections of Plateau region American Indian artifacts.

> **Address:** Campus Box 8096, 5th Avenue and Dillon Street, ISU
>   Building 12, Room 205C, Pocatello, Idaho 83209
> **Phone:** 208-282-3317
> **Web Site:** imnh.isu.edu

SPALDING

Nez Perce National Historical Park and Spalding Visitor Center   The Visitor Center has exhibits on Nez Perce history. There are numerous archaeological sites as well as an Indian agency cabin built in 1862 and Watson's store, which began as a trading post in 1911.

> **Address:** 39063 U.S. Highway 95, Spalding, Idaho 83540-9715
> **Phone:** 208-843-2261
> **Web Site:** www.nps.gov/nepe

Maryland

SUITLAND

National Museum of the American Indian Cultural Resources Center   For the most part, the American Indian materials collected by George Gustav Heye, the world's largest private collector of Native American artifacts, have been moved to the Suitland Cultural Resources Center. Tours are available.

> **Address:** 4220 Silver Hill Road, Suitland, Md. 20746
> **Phone:** 301-238-1435
> **Web Site:** www.nmai.si.edu

Massachusetts

CAMBRIDGE

Peabody Museum of Archaeology and Ethnology The Peabody Museum, started in 1866, houses a large collection of American Indian artifacts.

> **Address:** 11 Divinity Avenue, Cambridge, Mass. 02138
> **Phone:** 617-496-1027
> **Web Site:** www.peabody.harvard.edu

Montana

CHINOOK

Bear Paw Battlefield The Bear Paw Battlefield is the site of the final battle of the Nez Perce, where Chief Joseph surrendered.

> **Address:** 16 miles south of Chinook, Montana, on Cleveland Road (County Highway 240)
> **Phone:** 406-357-3130
> **Web Site:** www.nps.gov/nepe/pphtml/facilities.html

Blaine County Museum The museum has an exhibit on the Bear Paw Battle including a 20-minute audiovisual presentation.

> **Address:** 501 Indiana Street, Chinook, Mont. 59523
> **Phone:** 406-357-2590
> **Web Site:** www.chinookmontana.com/museum.html

PABLO

The People's Center The goal of the People's Center is to tell the story of the Salish, Kootenai, and the Pend d'Oreille.

> **Address:** P.O. Box 278, 53253 Highway 93 West, Pablo, Mont. 59855
> **Phone:** 406-883-5344
> **Web Site:** www.peoplescenter.org

WISDOM

Big Hole Battlefield The battlefield is a memorial to the Nez Perce War Battle of Big Hole in 1877.

> **Address:** P.O. Box 237, Wisdom, Mont. 59761-0237
> **Phone:** 406-689-3155
> **Web Site:** www.nps.gov/biho

New York

NEW YORK

National Museum of the American Indian George Gustav Heye Center The George Gustav Heye Center offers a number of workshops, tours, talks, and lectures as well as both permanent and temporary exhibitions.

Address: Alexander Hamilton U.S. Custom House, One Bowling
   Green, New York, N.Y. 10014
Phone: 212-514-3700
Web Site: www.nmai.si.edu

Oregon

EUGENE

**University of Oregon Museum of Natural and Cultural
History**   The museum has an extensive collection of Plateau Indian
artifacts.

Address: 1600 E. 15th Avenue, Eugene, Oreg. 97401
Phone: 541-346-3024
Web Site: natural-history.uoregon.edu

JOSEPH

Wallowa County Museum   The museum has displays that pres-
ent Wallowa County history, both of the Plateau Indians and white
settlers.

Address: 110 S. Main Street, Joseph, Oreg. 97846
Phone: 541-432-6095
Web Site: www.co.wallowa.or.us/museum

KLAMATH FALLS

Favell Museum of Western Art and Artifacts   The goal of the Favell
Museum is to reflect the West's heritage. There are more than 100,000
American Indian artifacts on display.

Address: 125 West Main Street, P.O. Box 165, Klamath Falls,
   Oreg. 97601
Phone: 541-882-9996

PENDLETON

Tamastslikt Cultural Institute   The institute opened in 1998 to pre-
serve the history of the Confederated Tribes of the Umatilla Indian
Reservation, the Walla Walla, Umatilla, and Cayuse. The Naami
Nishaycht Village is a living culture exhibit.

Address: 72789 Highway 331, Pendleton, Oreg. 97801
Phone: 541-966-9748
Web Site: www.tamastslikt.com

WALLOWA

Wallowa Band Nez Perce Trail Interpretive Center   The goal of the
center is to tell the story of the trail as well as the Nez Perce.

Address: P.O. Box 15, Wallowa, Oreg. 97885
Phone: 541-886-3101
Web Site: www.wallowanezperce.org

Pennsylvania

PHILADELPHIA

University of Pennsylvania Museum of Archaeology and Anthropology The museum has displays of American Indian culture and artifacts.

> **Address:** 3260 South Street, Philadelphia, Pa. 19104
> **Phone:** 215-898-4000
> **Web Site:** www.museum.upenn.edu

PITTSBURGH

Carnegie Museum of Natural History The section of anthropology at the Carnegie Museum of Natural History houses exhibits on a variety of American Indian cultures.

> **Address:** 5800 Baum Boulevard, Pittsburgh, Pa. 15206
> **Phone:** 412-622-3131
> **Web Site:** www.carnegiemnh.org/anthro/home.html

Rhode Island

BRISTOL

Brown University Haffenreffer Museum of Anthropology The museum is home to almost 100,000 artifacts of Native people around the country and the world.
> **Address:** 300 Tower Street, Bristol, R.I. 02809
> **Phone:** 401-253-8288
> **Web Site:** www.brown.edu

Washington

SEATTLE

Burke Museum of Natural History and Culture The museum's archaeology division has more than 1 million American Indian artifacts, including large collections of Columbia Plateau materials.

> **Address:** Box 353010, 17th Avenue NE & NE 45th Street,
>   University of Washington, Seattle, Wash. 98295
> **Phone:** 206-543-5590
> **Web Site:** www.washington.edu/burkemuseum

SPOKANE

Northwest Museum of Art and Culture The museum has one of the most extensive collections of Plateau Indian artifacts in the country, including 10,000 photographs of their life and culture.

> **Address:** 2316 W. First Avenue, Spokane, Wash. 99204
> **Phone:** 509-456-3931
> **Web Site:** www.northwestmuseum.org

YAKIMA

Yakima Valley Museum   The Yakima Valley Museum has exhibits of American Indian artifacts, focused on the Yakama Nation.

   Address: 2105 Tieton Drive, Yakima, Wash 98902
   Phone: 509-248-0747
   Web Site: www.yakimavalleymuseum.org

Washington, D.C.

National Museum of the American Indian on the National Mall   Opened in 2004, the museum's galleries and display spaces house both permanent and temporary exhibitions on the American Indian.

   Address: Fourth Street and Independence Avenue, S.W.,
      Washington, D.C. 20560
   Phone: 202-633-1000
   Web Site: www.nmai.si.edu

Further Reading

BOOKS

Daugherty, Richard D. *The Yakima People.* Phoenix, Ariz.: Indian Tribal Series, 1973.

Faulk, Odie B. *The Modoc.* New York: Chelsea House, 1988.

Gray-Kanatiiosh, Barbara A. *Modoc.* Edina, Minn.: ABDO, 2006.

Haines, Earl Shenck. *Indians of the Great Basin and Plateau.* New York: Putnam's, 1970.

Johnson, Michael, and Duncan Clarke. *Native Tribes of the Great Basin and Plateau.* Milwaukee, Wisc.: World Almanac, 2004.

Rifkin, Mark. *The Nez Perce Indians.* New York: Chelsea House, 1994.

Shaughnessy, Diane, and Jack Carpenter. *Chief Joseph: Nez Perce Peacekeeper.* New York: PowerKids, 1997.

Sherrow, Victoria. *Indians of the Plateau and Great Basin.* New York: Facts On File, 1992.

Simms, Laura. *The Bone Man: A Native American Modoc Tale.* New York: Hyperion, 1997.

Thompson, Linda. *People of the Plateau.* Vero Beach, Fla.: Rourke, 2004.

Time-Life Books. *People of the Western Range.* Richmond, Va.: Time-Life, 1995.

Williams, Jack S. *The Modoc of California and Oregon.* New York: PowerKids, 2004.

WEB SITES

Coeur d'Alene (Schitsu'umsh) Tribe. "Official Site of the Coeur d'Alene (Schitsu'umsh) Tribe." Available online. URL: www.cdatribe.org. Downloaded September 17, 2005.

Confederated Salish and Kootenai Tribes. "Official Website of the Confederated Salish and Kootenai Tribes." Available online. URL: www.cskt.org. Downloaded September 17, 2005.

Confederated Tribes of the Colville Reservation. "A Walk Through Time." Available online. URL: www.colvilletribes.com. Downloaded September 17, 2005.

"Kalispel Tribe of Indians." Available online. URL: www.kalispeltribe.com. Downloaded September 17, 2005.

Nez Perce Tribe. "Nez Perce Tribe Web Site." Available online. URL: www.nezperce.org. Downloaded September 17, 2005.

Index

Page numbers in *italic* indicate photographs/illustrations. Page numbers in **boldface** indicate box features. Page numbers followed by *m* indicate maps. Page numbers followed by *g* indicate tables. Page numbers followed by *t* indicate time line entries.

WITHDRAWN